The Disturbed Violent Offender

Hans Toch and Kenneth Adams

The Disturbed
Violent Offender

Foreword by Lloyd E. Ohlin

YALE UNIVERSITY PRESS   NEW HAVEN AND LONDON

Set in Baskerville type by Keystone Typesetting, Inc.
Printed in the United States of America by Vail-Ballou
Press, Binghamton, New York.

Library of Congress Cataloging-in-Publication Data
Toch, Hans.
  The disturbed violent offender / Hans Toch and
Kenneth Adams.
    p. cm.
  Includes index.
  ISBN 0-300-04533-6
  1. Violence. 2. Prisoners—Mental health. I. Adams,
Kenneth, 1953–   . II. Title.
RC569.5.V55T62 1989
364.3—dc20   89-5771
                                              CIP

The paper in this book meets the guidelines for
permanence and durability of the Committee on
Production Guidelines for Book Longevity of the Council
on Library Resources.

10   9   8   7   6   5   4   3   2   1

When I first read it this morning, I said to myself I never, never believed it before, notwithstanding my friends kept me under watch so strict, but now I believe I am crazy; and with that I fetched a howl that you might have heard two miles, and started out to kill somebody—because, you know, I knew it would come to that sooner or later, and so I might as well begin. I read one of them paragraphs over again, so as to be certain, and then burned my house down and started. I have crippled several people, and have got one fellow up a tree, where I can get him if I want him.

—Mark Twain, *Sketches New and Old*

Contents

Chapter 6

Chapter 7

Chapter 8

Chapter 9

Index, 179

Foreword

Major acts of violence are relatively rare events, but the public and media preoccupation with violence is endemic in our society. Violent crime episodes are a stable feature of prime time television, and headlines are quickly captured by shockingly violent victimizations. The fears such acts arouse are only partially assuaged by capture and punishment of the offender because the motivations and precipitating circumstances so often defy comprehension. Are these the unpredictable acts of deranged persons or those of hardened criminals exploiting crime opportunities at whatever cost to their victims? Who will be the next victims or how can that be prevented? If the offender is mentally ill, can he be cured? If crime is his way of life, can he be deterred?

In this volume the authors initiate a major attack on such questions. They do this not by elaborating apriori explanatory theories, but by undertaking detailed empirical analysis of the characteristics and experiences of the disturbed (mentally ill offenders) and the perturbed (criminal offenders) and those who are both. They argue effectively that it is impossible to develop useful sentencing practices or responsive treatment programs until the undifferentiated mass of violent offenders is broken down into more homogeneous groups that will invite more discriminating identification of causes and effects and more sensitive prescriptions for control. They are searching for patterns that sort violent offenders into groups with similar backgrounds, experiences, behaviors, and traits. The underlying assumption is that violent offenders pursue different careers driven by different internalized motivations and environmental pressures. The captions they attach to the groupings that emerge highlight differences in these motivations and pressures. A few illustrations may capture the diversity. They range from the impulsive burglar to the experienced burglar; the young explosive robber to the late career robber; the mature mugger to the disturbed sex offender; the chronic disturbed exploder to the acute exploder. Thus starting with a heterogenous mix of violent offenders, they employ the sophisticated statistical tools of cluster analysis to generate twenty-seven clusters or types of violent offenders.

At the outset the research team had to solve a difficult problem. Given the generally low rate of violent offenses against persons as compared to offenses against property; given the fact that most offenders engage in more than one type of crime; and given the need to identify the disturbed vs. perturbed offenders or those who are both, how was it possible to generate a sample that would adequately serve the goals of the study? They hit upon a strategy that worked remarkably well. They started out with a roster of new admissions to the New York State adult correctional system who had been sentenced to prison for a violent offense as defined by statute. They then matched these offenders with the computerized records of the state-operated psychiatric facilities and obtained a detailed service record. They then supplemented this information with facts obtained in the correctional intake and classification procedures and stratified the sample on the basis of the mental health information available for the purposes of analysis. The procedure is fully described in chapter 2, but is sketched here to note the ingenuity of a procedure that combines the record systems of two very different agencies to generate a sample that relies on different criteria of official processing and information gathering to set the sampling frame.

The clusters revealed not only different patterns of violence prior to the current imprisonment but also different dispositions toward violent behavior during confinement as well. The study permitted a follow-up of disciplinary and service records for the first two years of time served. Different patterns of coping with prison life were evident in the sample but the most disturbed created the worst management problems and required the most specialized services and hospitalization. The research team did not pursue the specific coping strategies in prison of the sample because they had accomplished this in an earlier study in considerable detail (Hans Toch and Kenneth Adams with J. Douglas Grant, *Coping: Maladaptation in Prisons* [New Brunswick, N.J.: Transaction Publishers, 1989]). In fact the current volume and the previous one on "coping" should be regarded as companion research reports that attack different aspects of the problems posed by violent offenders. In this volume, as noted above, a sample of admissions of violent offenders to the New York correctional system has been surveyed to create a typology of violent offenders that reveals a diversity of crime patterns prior to entering prison. This research lays the ground for devising more sensitive, responsive and effective sentencing, classification and treatment decisions by court and correctional functionaries.

In the prior study a sample of violent offenders released from the New York adult correctional system between July 30, 1982, and September 1, 1983, were analyzed from the standpoint of their mental health experience and disciplinary infractions while in confinement. The authors analyzed the patterns of misbehavior exhibited by these offenders, the patterns of pathology they displayed, and the special problems posed by patterns that reflected both disturbed and disruptive behaviors. A central concern was to develop a typology of coping strategies which they employed to survive in a prison environment. In this endeavor the authors developed a taxonomy of maladaption grouped under five headings "to describe the dominant goals the behavior patterns appeared intended to subserve" (p. 73). These were (1) gratifying impulses, (2) seeking refuge, (3) enhancing esteem, (4) pursuing autonomy, and (5) maintaining sanity. Each of these goals was further characterized by a number of subcategories reflecting thematic variations on the way different individuals sought to achieve these goals.

The insight and care which the authors have pursued in the

construction of the typologies to both research reports has resulted in a path-breaking contribution to the study and understanding of violent offenders inside and outside of prison. Before we can develop good theories we need good descriptive accounts of the matters to be explained. This is what this volume and its predecessor have accomplished in an original and stimulating fashion, because it opens the door to very important questions. It invites a further study that seeks to merge the typologies from both research projects to determine how behavioral clusters described in this volume enrich understanding of the coping strategies and behaviors these violent offenders exhibit in prison. Both of these studies relied on official records to create retrospectively the behavior and experiences of these offenders as stages in criminal and pathological careers. What is now needed are prospective longitudinal studies that disclose the processes and experiences that lead to the development of these career patterns and provide the data for theoretical analysis of cause and effect sequences. Finally there is a need to analyze further the policy implications of these findings and their application in sentencing and correctional decision making. In both books the authors have made constructive and insightful suggestions as to these implications and have also encouraged further study. The study and understanding of violent offenders has been greatly advanced by the work of this research team and the resourcefulness and imagination they have displayed in accomplishing it.

Lloyd E. Ohlin

Preface

For both authors this book represents the culmination of a learning experience. In my case this lesson has spanned decades, even though I had the benefit of wise mentors, chief among whom is a one-time colleague, Fritz Redl. Redl often started disquisitions about developmental difficulties by saying, "I want to highlight complexity." He was equally fond of noting that if textbook psychiatric patients had ever existed, they had become extinct—or virtually extinct.

Others to whom I should have listened were offenders and ex-offenders I met over the years, who offered lessons in complexity I did not digest. The principal lesson was that offenders can deviate not only from descriptions in criminology textbooks but also from portraits in other textbooks, such as those dealing with mental health problems. The Sturdy Professional Criminal is mostly a myth, as is the Neat Uncompounded Patient.

The culminating lesson I should have learned derives from Redl's studies of aggressive adolescents. These seminal studies have shown (among other things) that personal skills and deficits coexist in delinquents, as do discrepant dispositions and personality structures.[1] A tough predator by day can become a fearful

1. F. Redl and D. Wineman, *Children Who Hate: The Disorganization and Breakdown of Behavior Controls* (New York: Collier Books, 1962).

infant by night, and a notorious gang leader can become regressed and anxiety-ridden, without disjuncture or discontinuity. Complexity of this sort encompasses the cohabitation of paradoxical elements and requires a view of psychodynamics that links what at first blush looks inconsistent.

Such are lessons I should have assimilated, and I have a great deal of company in not assimilating them, particularly among "forensic mental health" experts, who deal with overlap between clinical and criminological problems and reliably underestimate it. One reason for this, I here suggest, may be our aversion to complexity in the shape of combinatory (crime-mental health) problems.

Other observers and I may also have been impatient because as social scientists we have a built-in penchant for cleaning up messes (data are invariably messy) and for trying to make sense of what we find as quickly as we can. My predilection as a psychologist has been for sorting groups of people into homogeneous subgroups that I felt I could understand. This enterprise is best expedited by starting with a neatly defined population, not by increasing heterogeneity (highlighting complexity) first, as Redl advised.

My research experience rests on two enterprises in which I have been involved over the years—one which studied violent offenders, and another which focused on mental health problems of prisoners.[2] Both enterprises consumed time and energy, and they were conceptually watertight. I now know that I must have ignored along the way, or brushed aside, evidence suggesting that my subjects in these studies overlapped, that vulnerable persons could and often did victimize other persons as they struggled to adapt.

I owe the change in my general approach to my colleague Ken Adams, who studied prison mental health from the perspective of guards. In the course of his work Adams noted that prisoners who received mental health services were often the most recalcitrant inmates and sometimes engaged in chronic misbehavior. This observation later inspired our first shared excursion into

---

2. See especially H. Toch, *Violent Men: An Inquiry into the Psychology of Violence* (Chicago: Aldine, 1969) and H. Toch, *Men in Crisis: Human Breakdowns in Prison* (Chicago: Aldine, 1975).

complexity, which centered on prisoners who had both mental health and behavioral problems in prison.

We decided early on to try to market a combinatory category that we called the Disturbed Disruptive Inmate. Armed with government money, we spent a full week at a motel with forty mental health and corrections staff, ranging from the head and the clinical director of a hospital and two deputy wardens through eight mental-health-unit chiefs, several clinicians and counselors, and a number of prison guards.[3] An illuminated sign at the entrance to the motel read "Welcome DDI Workshop." Passing motorists no doubt wondered whether we were concerned with deductible dental insurance or double-digit inflation. In the motel, however, our fellow-retreatants experienced no ambiguity and accepted (nowadays widely use) the acronym DDI with no doubt about its referent. These workers bought our concept because they all knew inmates who in their minds unambiguously qualified as both disruptive—posing disciplinary problems—and disturbed—manifesting semicontinuous mental health problems. The sorts of prison inmates who first came to our participants' minds were mostly extremes—legendary and infamous prison figures who were known (at least by reputation) to all staff in the system. These are the kinds of examples that seem to make definitions superfluous.

Consensus at the core of the problem is merciful, because at the outer reaches of the range—particularly when it comes to the question of whether individuals qualify as disturbed—there is a persistent lack of consensus. Whereas extremes require no definition, borderline cases discourage definition. Harmony is maintained by agreeing that where a specific person seems to need contact with mental health staff, or seems likely to benefit from such contact, little is to be gained by quibbling over whether the person's need—his vulnerability or his disequilibrium—transcends or fails to transcend an arbitrary diagnostic boundary.

My colleagues and I felt that if a definition of DDIs were in

3. The workshop was supported by Technical Assistance Grant FC-5, "Workshop on Disturbed, Disruptive Offenders" by the National Institute of Corrections, and by the New York State Office of Mental Health and Department of Correctional Services; the state agencies supplied release time and travel assistance to workshop participants.

order, we would like to work up to it rather than start with it. We wanted to begin with shared, plausible personal experiences. To this end, we asked our participants in the workshop to confer in advance with other staff and to enter nominations of disturbed and disruptive inmates. For each inmate nominee, we requested mental health and corrections dossiers. We distributed nine such dossiers to four- or five-person interdisciplinary task forces, whose mission it became to characterize their assigned inmates, highlight their motivational patterns, and track their careers through the corrections and mental health system. The sum of these group characterizations became our preliminary "definition"—the shared common ground on which further deliberations were premised.

Our subsequent task was to conduct a study of inmate difficulties in the prison, which we have reported elsewhere.[4] In this study we extended our inquiry, covering the widest possible range of maladaptive behavior among prisoners, with the extremes (DDIs) as the tip of our iceberg. We then grouped inmates according to the problems they seemed to manifest. Our hope was that our groupings now made more sense because we had liberated ourselves from constraints of the mind that resulted from the preclassification of people in terms of whether they *have* problems (are mental health clients) or *produce* problems (behave disruptively). Keeping such categories in suspension made the problem of human motivation messier, but we thought it might help to uncover psychological commonalities that we would otherwise miss.

The report that follows extends the logic of this approach from the prison to the community, and from misbehavior to criminal violence. The methodology we deploy on this occasion is new and different (we shall review it in detail), but our aim is the same—to enhance complexity before reducing it.

What we mean by complexity in this instance is denoted by the title of our book. Our concern is with serious (violent) offenders, but we shall assume that such offenders can also be persons who

---

4. H. Toch and K. Adams, with J. D. Grant, *Coping: Maladaptation in Prisons* (New Brunswick, N.J.: Transaction, 1989).

suffer from mental health problems (are disturbed). As the other side of the coin we are concerned with persons who have mental health problems (are disturbed), but we shall assume that such persons can also be serious (violent) offenders. The first enterprise is a criminological one and the second is psychological or psychiatric, but the combination allows for interdisciplinary questions.

Definitional issues that we shall face are analogous to those in our earlier study. At the extremes, our definitions will come easy but will be superfluous: A murderer is unquestionably a violent offender because he does serious personal harm; a psychotic in full bloom is by the same token "disturbed," given the floridity of his symptoms; a psychotic who commits murder is a "disturbed violent offender," given the consensus we find covering the significance of the person's crime and mental health status. The problem is that as we move from such extremes the definitions sit less easily and hang more loosely. This problem is particularly serious for mental health status, because violent offending is defined by statutes and ratified by courts, whereas mental illness is a seemingly evanescent, arbitrary line clinicians draw which bisects a continuum of behavior that ranges from exemplary adjustment to serious problems.

In the face of this dilemma we opt for inclusiveness, which permits us to define and undefine categories as the facts dictate. We shall at times describe disturbed VIOLENT offenders, where violence is indisputable and mental health status questionable, and DISTURBED violent offenders where the opposite obtains. Given inclusiveness, we shall encounter many persons who combine nonserious offenses with lower-order mental health problems, and conceptually we are interested in this spectrum where we find it. Public-policy issues will arise more narrowly, principally revolving around DISTURBED VIOLENT extremes and around relatively nonviolent but very disturbed offenders (the DISTURBED violent), who now suffer because they fall between the cracks of the system.

Our second strategy is to sort or group people as sensibly as we can on the basis of the information available to us. This task is atheoretical, though there are choices to be made about the attributes one considers in grouping. We must admit that *atheoretical* sounds inhospitable to thinking, but we feel that in practice it has the opposite impact, in that descriptive groupings permit wide ranges of speculation, including speculation from different disciplinary perspectives. This openness is particularly important where the persons we group are of interest to different specialities (such as criminology and psychology), in which observers have different concerns. The aim of typologizing hybrid persons as we see it must be to ensure that observers who have interests in different aspects of these persons can think about them more easily and compare them along attributes that are of concern to themselves and their colleagues. As it happens, such is a necessity for our study, given its clearly cross-disciplinary focus.

Another concern we have is that of public policy, to which we have already alluded. In this realm we contend that insensitivity to complexity is particularly fateful, because predefinitions force irregularly shaped human pegs into conventional holes—comprising services and institutions that do not accommodate those assigned to them. This matters because the harm reliably done in this way can be serious, not just to persons who are ill-served by settings, but to institutions that cannot accomplish their missions and to society at large.

Hans Toch

Albany
November 21, 1988

Acknowledgments

This book is based on research supported by the National Institute of Justice under Grant Number 85-IJ-CX-0044. We appreciate the confidence shown us by the Institute and the patience with which its project monitors (Helen Erskine and Richard Laymon) suffered through seemingly endless time extensions. We must emphasize, however, that opinions expressed in the following are ours, not those of the NIJ staff.

A study such as the one chronicled here requires a great deal of support from corrections and mental health personnel. We are fortunate in this regard and feel indebted for the good will we enjoyed and the assistance we received from many persons in the New York State Department of Correctional Services and Office of Mental Health. Among those who repeatedly facilitated our work are Raymond Broaddus, Joel Dvoskin, Ronald Greene, Frank Tracy, and Donna Mackey and her efficient staff.

Data collection and coding would have been a nightmare without the meticulous contribution of our long-term colleagues Gail Flint and Mary Finn, who dedicated much time to the agonizing details of this study. Sally Spring bore the burden of the report, including its numerous revisions, and preserved both her sanity and ours.

Chapter 8 was published in modified form as "The prison as dumping ground: Mainlining disturbed offenders," *The Journal of Psychiatry and Law* (Winter 1988). In connection with this version of the chapter, we are indebted for comments from Commissioner Thomas Coughlin, Joel Dvoskin, Ronald Greene, and Scott Christianson.

We are grateful to David McDowall, who helped along the way as consultant, and to Lloyd Ohlin and Gladys Topkis, who reviewed and improved the final manuscript. Professor Emeritus Louis L. McQuitty, whose thinking guided us when we mapped our research, passed away as we began our study. We miss him and regret his passing, and dedicate this book to his memory.

The Disturbed Violent Offender

Chapter 1

Introduction

A crime may capture glaring headlines for a number of reasons. The most obvious has to do with political salience, which is the reason drug-related crimes in particular get considerable publicity these days. There are also local concerns which are mobilized by circumscribed statistical spurts (or "waves") in certain types of offenses. For example, a community may see itself as engulfed by intoxicated drivers at one point or beset by men who steal and rape at another time, and such perceptions tend to translate into public demands for action.

There are also types of offenders that consistently stir the imagination, such as parolees who commit violent offenses, political conspirators and assassins, child abusers, citizens who kill police, and police who are criminally corrupt.

Another type of figure that consistently sparks public concern is the disturbed violent offender. This perpetrator is represented in headlines as an enigmatic person of inscrutable motives who picks his (or her) victims for private reasons and casually maims them or ends their lives. He is depicted as unreachable and unfeeling. Viewed in retrospect, he is an eccentric person who has led a life of fatally cumulating bitterness. If he has been seen by psychiatrists (as is often the case) the public wants to know why psychiatry failed—why tragedy was not foreseen and prevented.

Headlines that describe the disturbed violent offender (for example, "Fired Janitor Kills School Children," "Vet Goes on Rampage," "Ex-Patient Shoots Up Shopping Mall," "Sex Killer's Graveyard Yields Victims") paint an alarming portrait of a prevalent and serious problem. This problem is that of offenders who are arguably emotionally disturbed and thus may be both "mad" and "bad."

The headlines do both a service and a disservice. They are valid in the sense that the offenders they depict are unquestionably disturbed and indisputably violent. They are helpful in posing a question: how can we protect ourselves from dangerous persons who—some would tell us—belong in hospitals rather than prisons? Where the headlines fail, however, is in conveying the range of behaviors that characterize the mad and bad.

Many crimes committed by disturbed offenders are not headline-grabbing or bizarre and are, in fact, no different, or not very different, from offenses committed by nondisturbed offenders. There are also persons who lead double lives, in which chronic psychological problems and chronic offending coexist. Links between mental health problems and violence also vary: Some crimes of even the same person may appear "crazy" and others utterly "sane." Finally, some disturbed offenders may commit serious crimes, but there are many more whose crimes are ineffectual and largely nonserious.

Even such statements, however, must be made with caution. The subject of the disturbed offender is a tantalizing one—though admittedly depressing—but it is largely unexplored. This circumstance does not reflect a lack of interest or of thought. Rather, it is the result of a number of problems, many of which are substantial enough to make one refrain from treading where the terrain is possibly treacherous.

In the face of discouraging problems, we shall try to present a descriptive overview and typology of disturbed violent offenders and their offenses. This attempt will be tentative and exploratory because the task is indeed inhospitable. Lest the obstacles be underestimated, we begin in the remainder of this chapter by inventorying some of the conceptual and methodological traps that face us as we proceed.

Problems in Studying Disturbed Violent Offenders

When we started studying disturbed violent offenders we knew that we would be vulnerable to criticism, mostly on the grounds that our subject would be deemed illegitimately framed or our coverage indiscriminately inclusive. Such criticism is virtually inevitable, and to consider why, we must delve into the history of the field and into its present-day context.

The history of the topic is inauspicious. In the period when criminology and psychiatry were in their infancy, the field was rife with overgeneralizations about possible links between psychological abnormality and crime. To claim such links seemed particularly inviting in thinking about violent crime (especially murder) because the extremity of the behavior seemed to suggest extremity of motive. Clinical science at its inception also overestimated its reach. Psychiatrists who interviewed (and sometimes tried to treat) exotic offenders often implied that these offenders were, in essential respects, typical. These pioneers also espoused ambitious theories of crime causation, and their form of documentation—freely constructed case histories—made it impossible to disprove enticingly unfolded schemes.

To this day, there are studies of violence that include unverifiable observations. A popular book about murder, for example, details a single case which the author supplements with references to clinical experience, such as, "Having examined hundreds of people who have killed (and I exclude murders committed by organized crime), I have found that homicide usually does not originate because of a clearly defined impulse to murder, but is related to the intensity of inner conflicts,"[1] and "Eleven defendants charged with threatening the president or other government officials (of whom I examined eight and studied the records of two others) . . . all showed surprising similarities in their family background, their personality makeup and their pattern of behavior."[2]

Psychoanalytic theorists in particular have traditionally relied

1. D. Abrahamson, *The Murdering Mind* (New York: Harper and Row, 1973), 10.

2. Ibid., 18.

on case studies of patients to gain an understanding of their psychological functioning. In the United States this approach was first applied to offenders after the turn of the century under the auspices of the Juvenile Psychopathic Clinic in Chicago and by others, such as Bernard Glueck at Sing Sing Prison. In a seminal work published more than fifty years ago Franz Alexander and William Healy reviewed the personal histories of delinquent adolescents for "unconscious motives" rooted in childhood.[3] In an earlier volume, Healy had tabulated psychological and social variables ("factors") in the case histories of 823 repetitive juvenile offenders referred to his clinic by the Chicago juvenile court. Among other things, he found most of the delinquents to be disturbed.[4] In a more sophisticated book-length study Healy and Augusta Bronner examined paired cases of delinquent and nondelinquent siblings, using a matched experimental-control design. Healy and Bronner interviewed their subjects' parents and teachers and incorporated both these participants' perspectives in describing the interactions leading to the unfolding of delinquency.[5]

The earliest uses of case materials in forensic psychiatry were less disciplined and often reflected prevailing biases and preconceptions. This fact is illustrated by a "disorder" that was invented in the nineteenth century called Moral Idiocy or Moral Insanity (later dubbed psychopathy, sociopathy, and antisocial personality disturbance). This disease entity, according to an early textbook, was a brain defect leading to "more or less complete moral insensibility and absence of moral judgment and ethic notions" for which "treatment . . . is without prospect of success," so that "these savages in society must be kept in asylums for their own and the safety of society."[6] The case material that documented such pessimistic prognoses suggests to modern readers that the

3. F. Alexander and W. Healy, *Roots of Crime* (New York: Knopf, 1935).

4. W. Healy, *The Individual Delinquent* (Boston: Little Brown, 1914).

5. W. Healy and A. Bronner, *New Light on Delinquency and Its Treatment* (New Haven: Yale University Press, 1936).

6. R. von Krafft-Ebbing, *Textbook of Insanity* (Philadelphia: F. A. Davis, 1904), 623, 626.

diagnosis offered psychiatrists a way of expressing their disapproval of uninviting clients:

> She was lazy, mendacious, chasing after men, and given to prostitution. . . . She spent, in gourmandizing and amusements, money which her brothers and sister gave her. She did the same thing with what she earned, whether it was in service or by prostitution. . . . On account of her dissolute life she frequently had encounters with the police, for she offended public decency and gave no attention to police regulations. She found nothing improper in her manner of life. . . . She played the injured innocent, paid no attention to the regulations of the house, incited other patients to mischief, had constantly explosions of anger in her great irritability, always about her affair with the police. The police were her enemies, and tried to injure her, though she had never done wrong. Of her moral defect and her inability to direct herself she had no idea. . . . The patient is impossible, coarse to brutality, afraid of work, tries to persuade others not to work, goes about disturbing and scolding others, trying to attract men, and demands her discharge; but she cannot say what she will do when she is put at liberty. The patient was transferred to an institution for chronic insane.[7]

The creation of the concept of moral imbecility proved especially fateful because it was later used by diagnosticians to define obnoxious offenders as clinically nondisturbed. The content ascribed to the alleged disorder—a defect of the offender's conscience—invited this usage, making it a euphemism for congenital badness, malevolence, or antisocial character. In a recent book on mass murder, for example, the authors conclude:

> The serial killer . . . travels around, sometimes from state to state, searching for victims whom he can rape and sodomize, torture and dismember, stab and strangle. Even these truly sadistic killers are, however, more evil than crazy. Few of them can be said to be driven by delusions or hallucinations; almost none of them talks to demons or hears strange voices in empty rooms. Though their crimes may be sickening, they are not sick in either a medical or a legal sense. Instead, the serial killer is typically a sociopathic personality who lacks internal control—guilt or conscience—to guide his own behavior, but

7. Ibid., 627.

has an excessive need to control and dominate others. He definitely knows right from wrong, definitely realizes he has committed a sinful act, but simply doesn't care about his human prey. The sociopath has never internalized a moral code that prohibits murder. Having fun is all that counts.[8]

Many psychiatrists (including Benjamin Rush, a signer of the Declaration of Independence)[9] have held an assortment of views

8. J. Levin and J. A. Fox, *Mass Murder: America's Growing Menace* (New York: Plenum, 1985), 229–30.

9. Benjamin Rush (1746–1813) was physician general of Washington's Continental Army and became the "undisputed father of American psychiatry [whose] portrait adorns the official seal of the American Psychiatric Association" (T. S. Szasz, *The Age of Madness* [New York: Jason Aronson, 1974], 23). An example of Rush's penchant for taxonomy is the following: "When the will becomes the involuntary vehicle of vicious actions, through the instrumentality of the passions, I have called it *moral derangement*. [My prior discussion of] the morbid operations of the will are confined to two acts, viz., murder and theft. I have selected those two symptoms of the disease (for they are not vices) from its other morbid effects, in order to rescue persons affected by them from the arm of the law, and to render them the subjects of the kind and lenient hand of medicine." This passage dates from an 1812 publication (excerpted in Szasz, *Age of Madness*, 25). In the same essay, Rush prescribes "sober houses"—to be established "in every city and town in the United States"—for persons addicted to alcohol (26–27). Rush's favored techniques included a chair of his invention (the "tranquilizer") to which many parts of a patient's body could be strapped (E. Kraepelin, *One Hundred Years of Psychiatry* [New York: Philosophical library, 1962], 17), bursts of cold water to be poured down a patient's sleeves (64), and extensive bleeding. Rush was particularly fond of bleeding because he believed that "the cause of madness is seated primarily in the blood vessels of the brain" (quoted in F. G. Alexander and S. T. Selesnick, *The History of Psychiatry* [New York: Harper and Row, 1966]). Consequently, he felt that "to relieve the body of vascular congestion by bloodletting, by far the most common therapeutic measure of the day, would eliminate a basic cause of mental illness" (ibid.) There is evidence to suggest that Rush knew that the psychiatry of his day was primitive, "had a premonition that his methods would someday fall into disrepute," and wanted his impact on posterity to reflect a humane concern for the amelioration of suffering (ibid, 122–23).

The psychology of crime was Rush's long-term avocation. He delivered papers on prison reform in a seminar which ran under Benjamin Franklin's auspices, in which he advocated psychological sorting and differential treatment of prisoners, including medical treatment for offenders whose motives he adjudged to be pathological. Rush felt that all prospective convicts could be classified according to whether their crimes were inspired by "passion, habit, temptation or mental illness" (D. Fogel, *We Are the Living Proof* [Cincinnati: Anderson, 1979], 14).

that were surprisingly eclectic, and they favored classifying offenders into types, including groups to be treated medically. The evidence used by such alienists to classify offenders as normal or pathological, unfortunately, was often sketchy and prominently centered on the nature and/or severity of the offenders' crimes. At other times the material was a promiscuous assembly of data, permitting emphases to taste.

The historian David Rothman notes that the construction of comprehensive case histories such as those that to this day can be found in the folders of many offenders was designed to illuminate causes of difficulties so that individualized treatment programs could be designed for them. This approach reflected what Rothman describes as naive faith in science because it assumed that patterns would somehow emerge from comprehensive inventories of facts.[10] The result, however, has been precisely the opposite, in that biographical accounts contain some wheat but much chaff and offer no clues to which facts may be most characteristic or informative or causally relevant in individual instances.

More serious problems occurred as a result of high clinical expectations. The overblown claims of mental health experts had annoyed a generation of social scientists, who ended up by condemning the substance of the clinicians' concerns as well as their methods. Most early textbooks in criminology (written by sociologists reared in the hard-nosed positivistic tradition) ridiculed the notion that offenders could be seen as disturbed and took pains to stress the "normalcy" of crime—meaning *all* crime. This understandably parochial stance created a disjuncture in the field, whereby ruminations about crime causation diverged from clinical thinking, which was thereby denuded of criminological theory. Psychologists and psychiatrists who aspired to enter the "forensic" area were trained without benefit of crime-related expertise, while criminologists routinely dismissed offenders' mental health problems as having nothing to do with their criminal careers.

The reason this developing situation mattered was that clinical practitioners—particularly social workers, who for a time entered corrections in sizable numbers—interfaced blithely with delin-

10. D. Rothman, *Conscience and Convenience* (Boston: Little Brown, 1980).

quents, addicts, and disturbed offenders, applying their "main-line" clinical thinking, which criminologists had dismissed as not relevant to crime causation and hence, to recidivism. In time, criminologists and their allies—armed with masses of program evaluation data which showed that "nothing [that is, no treatment] works"—brought this activity into disrepute.[11] Clinicians continued to function in reduced numbers in correctional settings but were mostly seen as "mental health staff" or ameliorators of medical conditions, and no longer as rehabilitators of special groups of offenders.

To be sure, exceptions remained to the rule that mental health staff were not regarded as crime experts. These exceptions, however, were not contributions to clinical criminology. One exception was the demand that clinicians estimate the future probability of violent offenders' recidivism (dangerousness). The other exception involved the requirement that clinicians contribute to judgments as to the "sanity" of (mostly violent) defendants in courts. The former enterprise was inauspicious because many experts adjudged it to involve dubious extrapolations.[12] The sec-

11. The phrase derives from R. Martinson's article "What works?—questions and answers about prison reform" (*Public Interest*, 1974, *35*, 22–54). Martinson's conclusion was that "with few and isolated exceptions, the rehabilitative efforts that have been reported so far have had no appreciable effect on recidivism." A more recent summary of authoritative opinion based on review of the same data concluded that "at the present time, no recommendation about ways of rehabilitating offenders could be made with any warranted confidence, and, therefore, no new major rehabilitative programs should be initiated on a widespread basis. At the same time, neither could one say with justified confidence that rehabilitation cannot be achieved, and, therefore, no drastic cutbacks in rehabilitative effort should be based on that proposition." This conclusion was arrived at by a panel of social scientists convoked by the National Research Council (L. Sechrest, S. O. White, and E. D. Brown, eds., *The Rehabilitation of Criminal Offenders: Problems and Prospects* [Washington, D.C.: National Academy of Sciences, 1979], 102–03).

12. Some limitations have to do with the unreliability of clinical judgments, and others relate to the low probability of violent behavior, except among very chronic violent offenders. This low probability creates a problem because "events that have low base rates are very difficult to predict with high levels of accuracy. Moreover, even the accuracy that is achieved comes at the cost of high rates of 'false positives,' that is, persons who are predicted to be dangerous but who will actually not display such behavior" (S. A. Shah, "Dangerousness: conceptual, prediction and public policy issues," in J. R. Hays, T. K. Roberts, and K. S. Solway,

ond concern was not in fact intended to be scientific. However, testimony about insanity is an important activity because it lends the illusion of science to a distinction that must be made on unscientific grounds when one wishes to sort disturbed from nondisturbed offenders.[13]

The insanity defense provides a distracting criterion of crime-related emotional problems. The insanity defense originated as a way of ensuring that crazed assassins and other transparently demented offenders were not dragged, kicking and screaming, to the scaffold.[14] It is important to keep this goal in mind because it means that the concern was with avoiding farcical displays of punitiveness rather than with excluding disturbed persons in general from punishment. The point of the insanity defense was to define the limits of what one could sensibly call blameworthy conduct. This issue was important to judges, who resolved it by concluding that blame should not attach to any act committed by a person who did not know what he or she was doing while he or she was doing it. The earliest versions of this doctrine were formulated during the reign of Edward I (1272–1307).[15] Later, routine pardons were accorded to murderers classed as "lunaticks" because of "not knowing more than wild beasts"; historians further noted that "madness became a complete defense to a criminal charge" under the liberal auspices of Edward III (1327–77).[16]

The insanity defense preceded the advent of clinical science by

eds., *Violence and the Violent Individual* [New York: Spectrum Publications, 1981], 161).

13. Though insanity is a purely legal concept, one problem with the term is that colloquial and past technical usage broaden its connotations. The dictionary defines *insanity* as "a deranged state of mind" or "a mental disorder." These lay definitions correspond to vintage clinical definitions, as witnessed by the fact that the earliest house organ of the American Psychiatric Association was the *American Journal of Insanity,* which continued publication for many decades.

14. H. Weihofen, *Insanity as a Defense in Criminal Law* (New York: The Commonwealth Fund, 1933). A more contemporary perspective is that of Justice Bazelon, who wrote in the well-known *Durham* decision (see note 24 below) that "our collective conscience does not allow punishment where it cannot impose blame."

15. S. S. Glueck, *Mental Disorder and the Criminal Law: A Study in Medico-Sociological Jurisprudence* (Boston: Little, Brown, 1925).

16. R. M. Perkins, *Criminal Law* (New York: Foundation Press, 1957), 739.

several centuries. By 1843, however, when the contemporary insanity defense was formulated (the action was taken in an uproar over a case reminiscent of that of John Hinckley,)[17] medical evidence was introduced in the trial, as in others in which insanity had become an issue. The landmark case that sparked controversy was that of Daniel McNaghten, about whom physicians testified that he "labored under an insane delusion" that he was persecuted by (among others) the prime minister of England. McNaghten was acquitted "on the ground of insanity" of having shot and killed the prime minister's secretary, and the judges of England were challenged by indignant legislators to justify their verdict. The McNaghten doctrine, which defines insanity in many U.S. jurisdictions to this day, is annunciated in the key paragraph of the judges' reply:

> The jury ought to be told in all cases that . . . to establish a defense on the ground of insanity, it must be clearly proved that, at the time of committing the act, the party accused was labouring under such a defect of reason, from disease of the mind, as not to know the nature and quality of the act he was doing, or if he did know it, that he did not know he was doing what was wrong.[18]

Obviously the issue for the judges was not that the offender suffered "from disease of the mind"—though he had to be mentally disturbed for the definition to apply. The issue, rather, was that the offender must be oblivious to his actions or their impact as a result of being thus disturbed. This criterion is narrow and describes (a) a purely hypothetical, metaphysical state of mind which (b) is difficult for an observer to ascertain, particularly in retrospect. The criterion is also not spontaneously thought of by psychiatrists when they are left to their devices in dealing with

17. John Hinckley made an assassination attempt on President Reagan in which the president and a member of his entourage were injured. Hinckley was subsequently acquitted by reason of insanity under the American Penal Law Institute standard (see note 25 below), as adopted by federal courts in *United States v. Brawner* (471 F.2d 969, D.C. Cir., 1972). Hinckley's insanity acquittal sparked a public furor, and in partial reaction Congress tightened the insanity standard (in the Federal Crime Control Act of 1984), requiring "clear and convincing evidence" of incapacity and placing the burden of proof on the defense.

18. Weihofen, *Insanity as a Defense*, 28.

patients. Given the narrowness and diagnostic irrelevance of the rule, it is not surprising that physicians found it uncomfortable almost as soon as it had been formulated. Among others, the American psychiatrist Isaac Ray led a spirited attack on the insanity defense in the 1860s and convinced the courts in his home state of New Hampshire to expand the definition. Ray felt strongly that psychiatrists should be allowed to operate in an unfettered fashion, and should present evidence as they saw it as to the mental condition of the offender and its expected impact on his crime.

Isaac Ray was a founder of the American Psychiatric Association and has been called "by far the most influential American writer on forensic psychiatry during the whole nineteenth century."[19] Like other psychiatric critics of the McNaghten rule, Ray objected to the premium the rule placed on impairment of knowledge. He wrote,

> The error arises from considering the reason, or to speak more definitely, the intellectual faculties, as exclusively liable to derangement, and entirely overlooking the passions or affective faculties. . . . While the reason may be unimpaired, the passions may be in a state of insanity, impelling a man . . . to the commission of horrible crimes in spite of all his efforts to resist. . . . The whole mind is seldom affected; it is only one or more faculties, sentiments, or propensities, whose action is increased, diminished or perverted, while the rest enjoy their customary soundness and vigour. . . . True philosophy and strict justice require that the action of the insane should be considered in reference . . . to the faculties that are diseased.[20]

19. W. Overholser, "Isaac Ray, 1807–1881," in H. Mannheim, ed., *Pioneers in Criminology* (Montclair, N.J.: Patterson Smith, 1973), 177.

20. I. Ray, "Lecture on the criminal law of insanity," *The American Jurist*, 1835, *14*, p. 253. The same point has been made by many psychiatric spokespersons, including a committee for the Group for Advancement of Psychiatry, who wrote about the McNaghten standard that "the rules place a premium on intellectual capacity and presuppose that behavior is actuated exclusively by reason and untrammeled choice. On the one hand, this overemphasizes the importance of the intellect, reason and common sense; on the other hand, it underemphasizes the emotional pressures that energize behavior" (Group for the Advancement of Psychiatry, Committee on Psychiatry and Law, *Criminal Responsibility and Psychiatric Expert Testimony*, report no. 26 [Topeka, Kan., 1954], 4). Some psychiatrists disagree with this view. Carl Wertham, for instance, writes,

More fundamentally, Ray opined that insanity was either a fact or not a fact, and "properly speaking, there can be no law on this subject other than the facts themselves."[21] Ray felt that psychiatrists should be recognized as scientific experts and dismissed as irrelevant the circumstance that they often disagreed as witnesses (he wrote that "very little evidence of any sort is completely harmonious").[22] This position has recently been characterized as cavalier by such incisive critics as Thomas Szasz, who writes,

> It is possible, in virtually any case in which psychiatric testimony is introduced, to secure psychiatric testimony in opposition to it. How are we to reconcile this fact? If we compare psychiatric to, say, toxicological testimony, a comparable situation would be one in which the toxicologist for the prosecution testified that a body contained a lethal amount of arsenic, whereas the toxicologist for the defense testified that it did not. This, of course, never happens, because one of the experts could be, and would be, proved guilty of perjury. . . . Mental illness is not the sort of phenomenon whose presence or absence can, at least according to current practices, be easily identified by scientifically impartial methods. Since there are no scientifically accepted ethical and social criteria of mental health—a concept corresponding to the permissible level of arsenic in the human body in our analogy—there can be no scientifically accepted criteria of mental illness.[23]

Notwithstanding such criticisms, experiments with liberalized insanity definitions that give psychiatrists more elbow room have

---

The distinction between right and wrong is not a purely intellectual performance, but affects the whole personality and has definite and important emotional components. . . . So the rule inherently does include emotion and affect. . . . The law allows the psychiatrist to lay all the proof of the diagnosis and degree of a mental disease before the court. According to scientific psychiatry, that includes necessarily the emotional part of the personality. If the law singles out one criterion for its own purposes, that does not mean that the psychiatrist has to seal off that aspect from the rest of the affected personality (F. Wertham, *A Sign for Cain* [New York: Paperback Library, Coronet, 1969], 245).

21. Overholser, "Isaac Ray," 194.
22. Ibid., 192.
23. T. Szasz, "Criminal responsibility and psychiatry," in H. Toch, ed., *Legal and Criminal Psychology* (New York: Holt, Rinehart and Winston, 1961), 162–63.

been introduced. For a period of several years, for example, the District of Columbia used a standard (the *Durham* rule) which provided psychiatrists unlimited opportunity for unfettered testimony. The three-judge panel of the U.S. Court of Appeals (headed by J. Bazelon) wrote,

> We find that as an exclusive criterion the right-wrong test is inadequate in that (a) it does not take sufficient account of psychic realities and scientific knowledge, and (b) it is based upon one symptom and so cannot validly be applied in all circumstances. . . . We conclude that a broader test should be adopted. . . . The rule we now hold must be applied on the retrial of this case and in future cases is not unlike that followed by the New Hampshire court since 1870. It is simply that an accused is not criminally responsible if his unlawful act was the product of mental disease or defect. . . . The legal and moral traditions of the Western world require that those who, of their own free will and with evil intent, commit acts which violate the law shall be criminally responsible for those acts. Our traditions also require that where such acts stem from and are the product of a mental disease or defect as those terms are used herein moral blame shall not attach and hence there will not be criminal responsibility. The rule we state in this opinion is designed to meet these requirements.[24]

More recently the federal courts and a number of states have adopted a modified McNaghten rule which incorporates moderately liberalizing recommendations of the American Law Institute's *Model Penal Code.* This definition reads,

> A person is not responsible for criminal conduct if at the time of such conduct as a result of mental disease or defect he lacks substantial capacity either to appreciate the wrongfulness of his conduct or to conform his conduct to the requirements of the law.[25]

The insanity defense, however, remains in essential respects a circumscribed defense. It offers a legal—not a clinical—criterion designed to apply (and applied) to a small minority of very seriously disturbed offenders whose offenses are extreme.[26] The

24. *Monte W. Durham v. United States,* 214, F.2d 862 (D.C. Cir., 1954).

25. See note 17 above. The ALI proposal was first published in *Model Penal Code,* Proposed Official Draft (Philadelphia: American Law Institute, 1962).

26. R. Pasewark, "The insanity plea: A review of the research literature," *Journal of Psychiatry and Law,* 1981, *9*, 357–401.

existence of the rule helps make salient the question of whether these offenders are disturbed but otherwise creates a problem because it invites the presumption that the law distinguishes between disturbed offenders and nondisturbed offenders, as it largely does not. The critical fact is that the overwhelming majority of disturbed offenders are processed without the question of their sanity being raised. This does not mean that these persons' mental state is criminologically irrelevant or that their offenses are untainted by their condition. The fact that some offenders are adjudged "insane," however, creates the implication that all offenders not so adjudged must be "sane" persons who commit "normal" offenses.

Disturbed violent offenders are difficult to locate and to define. We can take it for granted that the violent offenders who are adjudicated not guilty by reason of insanity must first be disturbed offenders, but the group is small and presumably quite unrepresentative. Other disturbed offenders are dispersed in a variety of settings, and, once located, they are apt to present definitional problems in that cross-sectional and historical portraits may yield different admixtures of emotional problems, offenses, and violent behavior, particularly over time.

Mental health varies over a person's life span, and violent offenses take place at particular junctures in time, during which the person may be disturbed or nondisturbed. Even if the person is disturbed and commits an offense, however, this does not mean that the occurrence of the offense, its nature, or its quality is affected by the person's mental condition. Psychological problems, moreover, cover a wide range, and we have noted that a line between disturbed and nondisturbed is very hard to draw. Violence is also a spectrum, ranging from moderate to extreme and from sporadic to habitual.

If we define a disturbed violent offender as a person who is sometimes undeniably disturbed and who commits offenses involving violence, such a person may be located among mental patients at a given point in his life and among offenders at other points. The former fact has been a matter of concern because the admixture of disturbed violent persons and other disturbed persons may in the public mind stigmatize mental patients as violence-prone.[27] To neutralize this stigma some observers have stressed that mental patients appear to be more criminogenic than nonmental patients only statistically because mental patients who have criminal records are included in the calculations.[28] The implication is that these disturbed offenders are in fact mainline offenders who happen to be in hospitals but would look more at home in prisons.

A comparable point holds for offenders in the criminal justice system—particularly inmates in prisons—who turn out to have mental health problems that require attention. Observers note that such persons have frequently had problems in the community and have received services, including hospital services. This fact invites the charge that chronic patients become inmates because they are prematurely discharged or "dumped," landing in prisons by default.[29]

Neither crime-accentuating nor pathology-accentuating portraits accommodate the third possibility that many persons are

27. As has been pointed out by Shah ("Dangerousness"), this stigma is increased by involuntary commitment criteria which emphasize "danger to self and other," leaving the impression that persons are hospitalized because they are violence-prone. Shah writes,

> there is the implicit, sometimes even explicit, assumption that by virtue of being mentally ill a person is more likely to engage in dangerous and violent behaviors. . . . Commitment laws for the mentally ill seem to be premised on the assumption (actually a belief) that, as a group, the mentally ill constitute one of the most dangerous groups in our society. Yet there is no sound or convincing empirical evidence to support such a belief" (ibid., 168).

28. Actually, the statistic at issue is misleading. Hospitalized ex-offenders have higher arrest rates than the general population, but arrest rates for *violent* crimes of the group are similar to those of the population when both are compared to offenders released from prison (H. J. Steadman, J. J. Cocozza, and M. E. Melick, "Explaining the increased arrest rate among mental patients: The changing clientele of state hospitals," *American Journal of Psychiatry*, 1978, *135*, 816–20).

29. This charge is premised on another assumption, which is that disturbed persons in correctional settings have proliferated in proportion to inmate populations. This assumption is universally endorsed by jail and prison administrators but cannot be substantiated given (1) the paucity of trustworthy epidemiological surveys, and (2) disagreement about the definitions of mental illness one would

both legitimate patients and legitimate offenders and become legitimate clients of both systems, or of one or the other system at different points in time.

To be sure, all agencies may make an effort to exclude other agencies' clients. The insanity defense can be regarded as such an effort by the courts, as can the competency examination, which is designed to avoid criminal trials in which the defendant is so handicapped that he does not understand what is happening to him when he is tried.[30] Mental health programs in their turn can exclude offenders at intake (claiming lack of security or irrelevance of service) and may discharge patients with behavior problems as unacceptably "disruptive." There are also more complex and subtle screening procedures, which include rejecting multiproblem clients on the ground that they are better served elsewhere.

The issue of multiproblem clients is particularly germane to disturbed offenders because such offenders are often disadvantaged persons who manifest a variety of deficits. This observation is familiar to service providers today but could have been advanced decades ago because the sociologists' original case against the clinical approach was buttressed by statistics demonstrating that crime was associated with social disadvantages that were known to produce other undesirable consequences as well.

---

have to agree upon for epidemiological research to take place. One stumbling block, for example, is that rates can be inflated or deflated through the inclusion or exclusion of the "antisocial personality" construct (see note 1) as a formal diagnosis. In one prison survey, for example, 78 percent of male inmates were diagnosed as sociopathic (S. Guze, *Criminality and Psychiatric Disorder* [New York: Oxford University Press, 1976]).

30. Halleck points out that the doctrine of pretrial competency, which dates to the seventeenth century, is "fundamental to the integrity and dignity of the legal process" because "trying individuals who may not even understand why they are on trial is inherently absurd, as well as incompatible with the commitment to justice" (S. Halleck, *The Mentally Disordered Offender* [Washington, D.C.: National Institute of Mental Health, 1986], 20). Halleck also notes, however, that competency to plea bargain is rarely at issue. Given that the defendant is in theory a party to the plea bargain—which presupposes his active participation—the failure to raise the "competency" question at this key juncture is mystifying, especially since most criminal cases are resolved through guilty pleas, which presuppose plea bargains.

Shaw and McKay, of the pioneering Chicago Area Study, for example, ask,

> Many other "problem" conditions might be listed, each representing a state of affairs considered undesirable by most citizens. These would include various forms of unemployment, dependency, misconduct, and family disorganization, as well as high rates of sickness and death. It may be asked: Do these other phenomena exhibit any correspondence among themselves and with rates of boys brought into court?[31]

Shaw and McKay answer their own question affirmatively. They report very high intercorrelations among problems of persons who reside in the most disorganized neighborhoods of metropolitan areas, and conclude that "any great reduction in the volume of delinquency in large cities probably will not occur except as general changes take place which effect improvements in the economic and social conditions surrounding children in those areas in which delinquency rates are relatively high."[32]

The recognition that social disadvantages can produce multiple handicaps is important because it means not only that the same person can have two or more problems but that these problems can reinforce each other in a variety of ways. This fact has become increasingly obvious to scholars and is illustrated by changes in their perspective about causal links such as those between family problems, educational deficits, unemployability, and addiction, on the one hand, and delinquent careers, on the other.[33] The accommodation of contemporary criminologists to the possibility of increased complexity of causation is especially stimulated by longitudinal studies which permit them to order events in time so that they can trace antecedents and consequences in causal chains and loops.[34]

Such developments are helpful to our own inquiry, but the

31. C. R. Shaw and H. D. McKay, *Juvenile Delinquency and Urban Areas* (1942. Reprint. Chicago: University of Chicago Press, 1972), 90.

32. Ibid., 321.

33. T. P. Thornberry, "Toward an interactional theory of delinquency," *Criminology*, 1987, *25*, 863–91.

34. D. P. Farrington, L. E. Ohlin and J. Q. Wilson, *Understanding and Controlling Crime* (New York: Springer, 1986).

evolving sociological model does not include mental health problems, and it cannot do so because the proportion of offender populations who have such problems looks small. This means that whereas more prevalent deficits (such as drug addiction and school failure) can be plugged into criminological equations, emotional problems are likely to remain as noise in such equations, as long as they are narrowly defined.

Violence as a variable suffers from the opposite problem in that a good deal of the offense spectrum includes violence, which complicates the task of disentangling violent crime from nonviolent crime, except at extremes. Long careers are apt to be heterogeneous in the sense that they include both violent and nonviolent offenses.[35] The specialized "violent offender" is a rarity, and definitions of violent offenders must accommodate mixed careers that include repeated violent involvements. Even when this is done, however, the dependent variable in studies that use such definitions is more saliently the chronicity of crime than the violence of the offenses committed.

It is uninviting to think of people as both mad and bad. We have implied that the insanity defense is unpopular and has been controversial since its inception. One reason is that where harm is salient, the notion of exculpation (and escape from punishment) is uncongenial to the public. A second reason has to do with the connotations of crime and mental illness, which make these concepts hard to reconcile and combine.

One generally tends to equate crime with malevolence and illness with helplessness. Crime, therefore, invites resentment, and illness, sympathy. It is hard to summon up sentiments that contrast so sharply, assuming it were possible to envision malevolent helplessness (or helpless malevolence) as a target of feelings.

Combinations of madness and badness are also puzzling, and the mind rejects them. Fortunately, badness tends to be documented in most instances, while madness is at best postulated. The harm crime does is a tangible fact, whereas the offender's hypothesized disability is an issue that is often in dispute by

---

35. M. E. Wolfgang, R. M. Figlio, and T. Sellin, *Delinquency in a Birth Cohort* (Chicago: University of Chicago Press, 1972).

experts who assert and deny its existence. This makes it easy to resolve the problem of logical dissonance by classifying mad/bad persons as bad persons who are of somewhat eccentric dispositions and whose badness preempts our attention.

The problem is eased by sequencing of conduct. If a person behaves madly today and acts badly tomorrow he is not deemed mad/bad but mad-turned-bad. After the person offends he becomes an offender and can be dealt with as such. After the same person breaks down (provided he is not offending at the time) he becomes a patient, and we can again treat him.

The formula of personal transmutations is convenient, but it must often be applied in strangely compartmentalized ways. If symptoms are destructive or misbehavior is bizarre different aspects of the same act can invoke disparate responses in tandem. Deadpan punitiveness can precede therapy, or vice versa. This sequential process implies such assumptions as that treatment can restore the person-as-patient to a condition such that the person-as-offender can be punished. The person-as-offender can then become a person-as-patient as soon as his medication wears off and/or his punishment commences, as when the offender enters prison where he receives mental health services.

Recidivism studies support a segmented view of disturbed offenders. Offenders and patients, and combinations of the two (such as insanity acquittees, defendants adjudged incompetent, and disturbed offenders adjudicated as "dangerous"), have been tracked in follow-up studies to ascertain their rates of rehospitalization and reoffending.[36] One would think that such investigations would point to linkages between mental illness and crime, but the research has the opposite import, even where the persons studied are clearcut disturbed violent offenders when they become subjects of study.

This outcome of research is a combined effect of the facts that

36. The third category includes two "natural experiments," in which courts of appeal ordered the release of disturbed offenders who had been retained in prison hospitals because they had been adjudged dangerous a number of years earlier. The offenders did relatively well after they had been released into the community. See H. J. Steadman, and J. J. Cocozza, *Careers of the Criminally Insane* (Lexington, Mass.: D. C. Heath, 1974); T. P. Thornberry and J. E. Jacoby, *The Criminally Insane* (Chicago: University of Chicago Press, 1979).

are customarily unearthed in the studies (variables predicting one sort of recidivism or the other) and the approaches to the garnering of these facts (how one goes about recidivism research, which means locating variables that predict and denote recidivism).

Segmentation of the disturbed offender as subject occurs because reoffending is correlated with one set of facts—age, for instance, and type of offense—and rehospitalization with another set of facts.[37] Even where unquestionably disturbed offenders are followed into the community, different failures of members of the group can be traced to different predictors, making it appear that the group contains (a) chronic offenders who happened to be disturbed, (b) chronic patients who happen to have offended, and (c) a composite type of offender whose offense behavior and emotional problems exist side by side, responding to different drummers in compartmentalized ways.[38]

This bifurcated (or trifurcated) view of recidivism persists in reviews of research trends over time. When we compare newer studies with older studies, we see more recidivism reported among patients.[39] As we have implied, this trend is then custom-

37. The three classic variables that predict offender recidivism are age, prior criminal record, and present offense (see V. O'Leary and D. Glaser, "The assessment of risk in parole decision making," in D. West, ed., *The Future of Parole* [London: Duckworth, 1972]). Among the variables that predict rehospitalization are age, past mental illness, marital status, and diagnosis (E. Zigler and L. Phillips, "Social competence and outcome in psychiatric disorder," *Journal of Abnormal and Social Psychology*, 1981, *63*, 254–71; W. Schofield, S. Hathaway, D. Hastings, and D. Bell, "Prognostic features in schizophrenia," *Journal of Consulting Psychology*, 1954, *18*, 155–66; W. Morrow and D. Peterson, "Follow up of discharged psychiatric offender," *Journal of Criminal Law, Criminology and Police Science*, 1966, *57*, 33–34).

38. Two authors who represent this view write that "the correlates of crime among the mentally ill appear to be the same as the correlates of crime among any other group: age, gender, race, social class, and prior criminality. Likewise, the correlates of mental disorder among criminal offenders appear to be the same as the correlates of mental illness among other populations: age, social class, and previous mental illness" (J. Monahan and H. Steadman, "Crime and mental illness: an epidemiological approach," in N. Morris and M. Tonry, eds., *Crime and Justice: An Annual Review of Research*, vol. 4 [Chicago: University of Chicago Press, 1983], 181).

39. Among the earlier studies, which show lower rearrest rates, are M. C. Ashley, "Outcome of 1,000 cases paroled from the Middletown State Homeo-

arily attributed to an influx of Group 1 Persons (offenders) whose advent among nonoffending patients gives them a bad name. Contemporary prisons are similarly characterized as increasingly permeated with Group 2 Persons (patients), and the past absence of patients is seen as accounting for the fact that early studies showed no disproportionate pathology among prison inmates.[40] Recidivism statistics as data also pose a special problem for disturbed violent offenders because the form of violence most likely to be associated with pathology (non-felony-related) is relatively nonrecidivistic.[41] The violent offender thus invites being classed

---

pathic Hospital," *State Hospital Quarterly*, 1922, *8*, 64–70; H. M. Pollock, "Is the paroled patient a menace to the community?" *Psychiatric Quarterly*, 1938, *12*, 236–44; H. Brill and B. Malzberg, *Statistical Report of the Arrest Record of Male Ex-Patients, Age 16 and Over, Released from New York State Mental Hospitals during the Period 1946–48* (Albany: New York State Department of Mental Hygiene, Albany, 1954) (American Psychiatric Association, Mental Hospital Service Supplementary Mailing 153. August 1962); and L. H. Cohen and H. Freeman, "How dangerous to the community are state hospital patients?" *Connecticut State Medicine Journal*, 1945, *9*, 697–700. Among later studies, which show higher rearrest rates, are J. R. Rappeport and G. Lassen, "Dangerousness—arrest rate comparisons of discharged mental patients and the general population," *American Journal of Psychiatry*, 1965, *121*, 776–83; J. R. Rappeport and G. Lassen, "The dangerousness of female patients: A comparison of arrest rates of discharged psychiatric patients and the general population," *American Journal of Psychiatry*, 1966, *123*, 413–19; J. M. Giovannoni and L. Gurel, "Socially disruptive behavior of ex-mental patients," *Archives of General Psychiatry*, 1967, *17*, 146–53; A. Zitrin, A. S. Hardesty, and E. T. Burdock, "Crime and violence among mental patients," *American Journal of Psychiatry*, 1976, *133*, 142–49; and J. R. Durbin, R. A. Pasewark, and D. Alberts, "Criminality and mental illness: A study of arrest rates in a rural state," *American Journal of Psychiatry*, 1977, *134*, 80–83.

40. One well-informed researcher concludes that "the literature, albeit methodologically flawed, offers at least modest support for the contention that the mentally ill are being processed through the criminal justice system" (L. Teplin, "Managing disorder: Police handling of the mentally ill," in L. Teplin, ed., *Mental Health and Criminal Justice* [Beverly Hills: Sage, 1984], 54). On the other side of the fence, researchers contend that "mental hospitalization is an ever increasing occurrence for those with histories of criminal activity" (J. Cocozza, M. Melick, and H. Steadman, "Trends in violent crime among ex-mental patients," *Criminology*, 1978, *16*, 317–34, p. 330.

41. See O'Leary and Glaser, "The assessment of risk; also, G. Kassebaum, D. Ward, and D. Wilner, *Prison and Parole Survival: An Empirical Assessment* (New York: Wiley, 1971).

as a Type 2 (disturbed) or Type 3 (mixed, compartmentalized) phenomenon, which is why psychiatrists are invoked to predict "dangerousness" not illuminated by statistics.

Settings may recognize complexity but may not label it. One assumes that practitioners cannot avoid facing "mixed" client problems and dealing with them. Schools, for example, must manage students who are not only disruptive and disturbed but obviously disruptively disturbed or crazily disruptive. Although recognition of such problems is inevitable in the front lines, administrative considerations may constrain classifications of problems, which means that perceptions need not translate into veridical labels.

Classifications of people very often become by-products of resource allocation. In schools, for example, the proportions of students with misbehavior problems as opposed to mental health problems may be adjusted to accord with programmatic emphases in campaigns against problem areas such as truancy, drug use, vandalism, suicide, and educational deficits. In this sort of calibration adding mental health staff expands the pool of mental health clients and shrinking services reduces the pool. One can also try to ignore one's resources and expand or contract labels of people as one thinks they are needed, as in smoking/nonsmoking sections of airplanes. In some large jails, for example, the numbers of "mental health beds" vary from count to count, with services and facilities remaining roughly the same.

Such taxonomic exercises can be a problem because operational definitions can be enacted which bear no resemblance to the substance of real client needs. In jails, for example, mental health problems are almost always equated with suicide potential.[42] This means that an inmate who talks about killing himself (that is, who expresses what clinicians call suicidal ideation) may be attended to, while prisoners who are less obtrusively disturbed are neglected. The strategy could be defensible if its aim were to address inmate despondency, but the goal—suicide prevention—

42. J. J. Steadman, D. W. McCarty, and J. P. Morrissey, *Developing Jail Mental Health Services: Practice and Principles* (Washington: National Institute of Mental Health, 1986).

is one of controlling undesired behavior rather than improving mental health.[43]

Suicide poses issues of consequence because it reflects societal ambivalence about madness and badness. Szasz points out that suicide attempts had been historically defined as violent crimes, but the insanity concept redefined the behavior as mental illness.[44] Similar redefinitions occur when persons are committed to psychiatric settings, given that the prevailing hospital entrance requirements (danger to self or others) specify social harm but treatment targets symptom reduction. To reduce the person's symptoms may reduce his dangerousness, but if this occurs it is a corollary of more significant achievements such as restoring the person's contact with reality and ability to care for self. Mental health concerns, such as Can this person feed and clothe himself? Can he follow a daily routine? Can he lead an independent existence? Can he relate to other people? have little to do with dangerousness, which defines treatment candidates at entrance or discharge.

The situation is one in which mad/bad persons are defined as mad or bad at different junctures in time, or in contact with different agencies, or to subserve different aims. The result is humpty-dumptyish in the sense that there is no integrated approach to the person as a whole. The situation also impedes the reconstruction of lives that cannot be understood unless we recognize the contribution of pathology to the genesis of misbehavior.

Describing Mad/Bad Careers

We have suggested that there are difficulties in thinking about disturbed violent offenders as subjects of research. Some of these

43. H. Toch, *Men in Crisis* (Chicago: Aldine, 1975). A sad fact which makes the practice ironic is that despondent inmates who are isolated through suicide prevention in jails often experience exacerbated difficulties, including completed suicides.

44. T. Szasz, "Insanity and irresponsibility: Psychiatric diversion in the criminal justice system," in H. Toch, ed., *Psychology of Crime and Criminal Justice* (New York: Holt, Rinehart and Winston, 1979), 139–41.

difficulties are conceptual and others are strategic. Conceptual difficulties can compound strategic difficulties, and this makes it necessary for a researcher to operate atheoretically at first, holding conceptual problems in abeyance. One must arrive at and adhere to operational definitions that lead to an internally consistent picture, though broader questions relating to the nature of crime (or violence) and mental illness remain temporarily unresolved.

One set of definitions one must arrive at has to do with the population one will study. The subjects must be violent and disturbed, but few persons are adjudged violent and disturbed at the same time. This means that the researcher must select one variable that is contemporary and that describes the person's status while making do with a second variable that mainly describes his or her history. One must view persons who are currently definable as mad and/or bad, with records of madness and/or badness. Different selection strategies yield different subpopulations with different attributes.

Each variable (violent crime and mental health) yields interrelationships, but one variable (violent crime) is primarily dependent in that it can be affected by the other variable (mental health) but is unlikely to affect it. Given the one-way nature of this relationship, offender status makes a more plausible criterion or outcome measure, and mental health status makes a less plausible one. This consideration suggests that we might start an inquiry with a population of violent offenders whose mental health (as well as criminal) histories are available for review. The strategy has become increasingly feasible nowadays because mental health systems keep computerized records of the services they deliver to their clients.

Irrespective of which selection strategy one uses, one must recognize that definitions of madness or badness—official designations of offender and patient status—describe the responses of agencies as well as the behavior of the persons responded to by the agencies. One can at times correct for artificial definitions (for instance, one can independently assess the violence level of behavior by using descriptions of offenses), but one cannot escape the fact that a criminal conviction or a diagnosis is a judgment, not a behavior description.

Links between crime and mental illness are even more hypothetical since they represent assumed relationships between assumed categories of behavior. Coexistence of observed behavior is a safer criterion. One can describe temporal patterns, starting with the premise that behavior classifications that coincide in time or rapidly follow each other provide clues to interrelatedness, and that more extended sequences provide more enduring cues, having to do with behavioral consistencies (if any) over time. The study of consistencies over time must also be a core concern of consequential motivational research because personality, as conventionally defined, means no more and/or no less than consistency of behavior.[45]

The inferences one can draw from one's research in this area depend on the range of behavior, particularly of "mental health problems," one can subsume. Restricted definitions are always neater but tend to describe extremes or (at worst) exotica. Moreover, neatness dissipates in longitudinal portraits given the checkered careers of the subjects one studies—and mental careers are no less checkered than offense careers, which means that persons who at times are psychotic at other times manifest less serious disabilities with greater frequency. A more substantial argument against a restricted-range model is that it obfuscates the multi-problem nature of disabilities, which is already obfuscated by preclassifications of clients and the segmentation of services.

The liabilities of extended-range sampling (such as lack of precision) can be neutralized by sorting, grouping, or disaggregating populations in consequential ways. This fact is an asset to the multidimensional perspective we favor because we must sort disturbed violent offenders into groups for other reasons, such as the fact that our variables of interest (mental illness and violence) can intersect in many and diverse ways. We must also group people because the key questions we shall speculate about are ultimately motivational (for instance, How does mental illness

45. G. W. Allport, *Pattern and Growth in Personality* (New York: Holt, Rinehart and Winston, 1961).

affect offense behavior?), and to answer such questions one must get as close to the individual as possible while preserving the capacity to generalize to other persons.

"Consequential" disaggregation means that one must strive to select distinguishing attributes that have relatively substantial explanatory power, given the limitations of one's data set. Purely descriptive variables (such as the physical attributes of an offense) are probably dispensable because they carry only situational or criminalistic significance. And other recorded data (such as legal offense descriptions) must be beefed up to more closely approximate qualitative differences among persons or their behavior.

Disaggregation yields subgroups or typologies—in this case, types of offenders who differ in the combination of problems (violence and mental illness) they manifest. It probably is not critical whether one starts with subgroupings along one or the other of these problem areas because either sorting procedure (variations of violence across mental health groupings, or types of mental health problems across offense groupings) would permit us to review representative clusters of contrasting offenders.

One reason we have placed a certain emphasis on the past history of offenders is that we feel research exploring links between categories of behavior makes most sense if it can trace these links over time. In part this is so because sequences can illuminate changes from one behavior category to another. In particular, we see no way other than through a review of lives over time to describe the paradoxical sequences of destructiveness and non-resilience that may be represented among offenders who are at times violent and at times disturbed.

There is an additional virtue in combining typological and longitudinal views. When we portray grouped persons longitudinally, we ask not only, What sorts of problems do people have? and How do people's problems evolve? but also How do persons with different problems experience the evolution of their problems? and How do people whose problems evolve differently differ from each other?

Though such ways of posing differentiating questions are similar, they are also different. The first strategy involves preclassifying problems and tracking their course over time. In educational research, students can be divided into good students and poor students on the basis of averaged academic performance; next, typical histories can be charted. Poor students may be found to have short scholastic careers which begin inauspiciously and degenerate. Should this be so, we draw causal inferences, such as, Chances are, failure breeds failure.

Pure scientists delight in such inferences, but policymakers may need more discriminating data. The educator may have to ask questions (such as, "Which students offer hope or justify taking risks?) that call for closer scrutiny of career patterns. The same holds for reformers or interventionists, who need clues (such as spurts in desirable or undesirable behavior under specifiable conditions) to the impact of remedial interventions.

Such concerns increase the attractiveness of "career-based typologies" which use behavior trends as the basis for sorting people. This grouping strategy invites one to examine, for example, the downhill or uphill careers of students viewed separately, or the careers of chronic versus nonchronic offenders. The strategy does have "applied" advantages—for instance, it helps assess risk level where chronicity is predictive of difficulties. The approach also offers a way of posing questions about cause and effect sequences. By the same token, some questions become more difficult to ask when we concentrate on sequential (when) events and underemphasize content (what) concerns. It becomes harder, for example, to beome aware of latent or qualitative shifts—chronics, for example, keep looking chronic, though they have problems that change complexion over time.

The nondifferentiation of problem content is a particularly serious issue when we know that "the problem" is a composite set of difficulties that vary independently. We know of our disturbed violent offenders, for example, that they have *at least* two problems (mental illness and a propensity to aggress) whose manifestations can be traced separately. This knowledge almost forces us to inject problem-related criteria of disaggregation (What are the person's precise difficulties?) into our career typology (How does the person manage over time?) to produce a composite portrait (How do the person's varying problems change over time?).

When we engage in this sort of compounded exercise we obtain a more differentiated but also more cluttered picture of career patterns. In mitigation of this lack of neatness we can offer only the prospect of viridicality, a sense of variegated permutations of "real life" careers. We can also claim a somewhat innovative perspective which describes a range of serious and complex offenders in a way different from the averaged portraits customarily found in the criminological literature.

Chapter 2

Research Strategy

Newspaper headlines proclaiming "epidemics" of violence and of mental health problems or announcing the existence of yet another "crazed" murderer can give the impression that a large percentage of the population is violent or mentally ill. While the salience given to such stories reflects the high level of concern society attaches to these problems, it belies the fact that from a researcher's point of view serious violent crime and serious mental disorder are relatively infrequent events. National data collected by the Federal Bureau of Investigation indicate that in 1985 about six violent crimes were reported to the police for every one thousand persons in the general population.[1] Epidemiological estimates of mental disorder are harder to come by on the national level, but the evidence suggests that about 5 percent of the population have experienced serious mental illness such as schizophrenia, major depression, and manic episodes at some point in their lives.[2] In developing our approach to

1. Katherine M. Jamieson and Timothy J. Flanagan, eds., *Sourcebook of Criminal Justice Statistics—1986,* U.S. Department of Justice, Bureau of Justice Statistics (Washington, D.C.: U.S. Government Printing Office, 1987), 154.

2. L. N. Robins, J. E. Helzer, M. Weissman, H. Orvaschel, E. Gruenburg, J. D. Burke, and D. A. Regier, "Lifetime prevalence of specific psychiatric disorders in three sites," *Archives of General Psychiatry,* 1984, *41,* 949–58.

studying mentally disordered violent offenders we had to deal with this statistical reality.

Since our interests lie in persons who qualify as both mentally ill and violent, we could anticipate that difficulties inherent in a study of uncommon events would be exacerbated. The challenge we faced in designing our research was that of insuring a sample of mentally disordered violent offenders sufficiently large for multivariate statistical analyses while working within real-world limitations, such as the usual constraints on resources and time. Given these considerations, we could rule out a number of design strategies. For example, we could eliminate a design in which we randomly sampled from an arrest population, given that a study of 1,382 police-citizen encounters uncovered only three incidents in which violent crimes were committed by persons who showed evidence of mental disorder.[3] We could increase the yield of this type of selection process by focusing on a more restricted population, such as a group of mentally disordered individuals or a group of violent offenders, but the evidence suggests that the improvement would be marginal. A recent follow-up study of 3,858 mental patients found that only 50 of them were arrested for a violent crime within nineteen months of discharge to the community.[4]

What is needed, then, is a reliable and efficient procedure for identifying a substantial number of mentally disordered violent offenders. One such approach starts with a group of convicted violent offenders, then narrows it to those who have had recourse to mental health services. This procedure gives us a pool of recently violent individuals who at some point in the past may have been mentally ill. We can then refine our categorization of offenders as mentally disordered by collecting information on the nature and extent of services they had required.

Selection of the Sample

We began our sample selection with an entry cohort of inmates sentenced to a term of incarceration in the New York prison

3. This figure does not include traffic-related incidents. See L. Teplin, "Criminalizing mental disorder: The comparative arrest rate of the mentally ill," *American Psychologist*, 1984, *39*, 799.

4. Steadman et al., "Explaining the increased arrest rate."

system after having been convicted of a violent offense. During the time period that defines the cohort we reviewed—January 1985 through December 1985—12,764 offenders were admitted to the prison system.[5] Of this group of offenders, 8,379 were sentenced for a statutorily defined violent offense, a criterion that covers a wide range, including some burglaries.[6]

Our next step was to match the names and birthdates of the violent offenders in the cohort against computerized client records maintained by the New York State Office of Mental Health.[7] The records are a historical listing of persons who received outpatient or inpatient treatment at any state-operated psychiatric facility, thereby providing an efficient screening device for identifying persons with a history of admission to psychiatric service. The comparison yielded a total of 1,833 matches, which means that 22 percent of the entering prisoners had experienced some contact with the state mental health system. Having identified the former patients and secured their client identification numbers, we then accessed computerized service delivery files and obtained a treatment history of each individual. The treatment information, which includes date, type of facility, and type of service, would later be used to infer the nature and severity of mental health problems.

Upon examining the service delivery records, we found that most (66 percent) of the offenders had been forensic (court-referred) clients, for whom there was little or no treatment infor-

5. The prison intake cohort includes only new admissions. It does not include offenders returned to prison for violating parole.

6. We used the statutory definition of violent offense, which includes a few crimes that traditionally might not be considered violent. In New York State, degrees of burglary are distinguished by whether there was threat or physical harm to a victim (McKinney's Consolidated Laws of New York, Annotated, Book 39, Penal Law, Volume Sections 140 to 219, pp. 35–51 [St. Paul: West Publishing, 1975]). Legally defined violence extends to some property offenders because they may have threatened or harmed a victim. In addition, we note that the statutory definition of violence is the criterion that determines which criminals qualify for penalty enhancements under specialized violent offender laws, and the extension of these penalties to include some property crimes again reflects a concern for the violence potential of these offenses.

7. Cross-referencing of computerized corrections records and mental health records was done on the basis of last name, first two letters of first name, and date of birth.

mation. This picture contrasted sharply with that of the civil psychiatric patients we identified, who for the most part had extensive treatment records. We also found that a significant number of offenders had been admitted to psychiatric facilities for alcohol and drug abuse problems. This finding was particularly interesting to us, since the relationship of substance abuse disorders to violence could plausibly differ from the dynamics of other emotional disorders.

At this point in our sampling procedures we had identified a group of "mentally disordered" violent offenders with the following characteristics: (1) most of the offenders were forensic patients for whom we could not otherwise confirm a history of serious emotional disorders; (2) some offenders had received psychiatric treatment primarily for alcohol and drug abuse problems, and since substance abuse treatment programs also are run by paraprofessionals in quasi-therapeutic settings, inmates who were exclusively clients of these programs were not identified; and (3) the group did not include offenders who had received services in private psychiatric facilities only. In view of these considerations, we turned to another source of data—the correctional files—in order to refine our classification procedures.[8]

The New York State Department of Correctional Services maintains a file on each inmate at its central administrative office. The files contain a variety of records, many of which relate to the

8. Psychiatric patients who have serious drug or alcohol abuse problems are one example of the multiproblem mental health client. A recent newspaper article documents the fact that the mental health system has difficulty treating persons with combined psychiatric and substance abuse problems. The article notes that between one-fifth and one-half of the mentally ill are substance abusers, and a state commission estimated that there are one hundred thousand such dually disabled persons in New York. Even though an effective treatment strategy has yet to be developed, mentally ill substance abusers consume a disproportionate share of mental health resources. In the article, the father of a schizophrenic alcoholic is quoted as complaining, "The alcoholism programs can deal with alcoholism. The mental health programs can deal with mental illness. But my son has both and they don't know how to deal with that." At least one reason for this situation is that treatment approaches of alcoholism programs, which are often confrontational, and of psychiatric programs, which often use drugs supplemented by emotional and social support, can be incompatible ("Mental health system fails alcoholics, drug abusers," Albany *Times Union,* March 13, 1988, pp. A–1, A–4).

inmate's prison experiences. Of particular interest to us were documents generated during the intake and classification process that detail the offender's past mental health involvements and his or her criminal history. These records offered us another source of information on the offender's psychiatric history along with a complete chronology of adult criminal justice experiences.[9] However, since the information contained in these documents could be retrieved only manually, it was impractical for us to collect data on the entire offender cohort. We therefore invoked a sampling strategy, selecting all offenders with civil psychiatric records, a total of 625 inmates, for inclusion in the sample.[10] We also randomly sampled from the group of forensic patients we had identified (sampling ratio 1:7; n = 145) and from inmates with no record of treatment by the state Office of Mental Health (sampling ratio 1:12, n = 540). As we reviewed the correctional files, we abstracted information on mental health contacts and on participation in community substance abuse programs, later merging these data with the Office of Mental Health records and eliminating redundant entries in terms of date of contact and name of treatment institution. In addition, while searching the files, we coded the chronology of each offender's criminal history (dates and offenses) and the details of the violent incident for which the inmate was sentenced.

By invoking the correctional files as a source of information, we clarified the nature of treatment involvement for some forensic patients, and we uncovered some mental health clients who had not been identified by the computerized record search. In table 2.1 we display the composite treatment histories (correctional files and mental health files) by the initial classifications (forensic, civil, no service) derived from mental health files. We were able to confirm the treatment status of nearly all (99 percent) civil patients, which includes a substantial proportion (21 percent) who were treated for combined addiction–mental health problems. In

9. Many prison files contained information on juvenile offenses. We coded this information whenever available, recognizing that it may be missing for some offenders on account of laws that order juvenile records sealed as confidential.

10. We also included the handful of patients with extensive forensic treatment records in this group.

Table 2.1. Results of search for service delivery information by initial classification of mental health experience of offender

Service delivery based on correctional and mental health files	Initial classification of mental health experience		
	No history (n = 540)	*Forensic patient (n = 145)*	*Civil patient (n = 625)*
Psychiatric evaluation only	7%	13%	1%
Substance abuse treatment program	8	8	5
Psychiatric treatment program	15	22	73
Psychiatric and substance abuse treatment programs	2	2	21
No service delivery information	68	56	0

contrast, we were less successful with the forensic clients, failing to locate any service delivery information on more than half (56 percent) the group. We infer from this absence of information that treatment experiences were minimal and that these clients probably did not suffer from serious disorders. We were, however, able to discern that some forensic patients participated in treatment programs (22 percent) or had undergone psychiatric evaluation (13 percent) only. The figures on the group initially described as having no service history are interesting because they bear on the advantages of accessing multiple sources of information. For more than two-thirds of this group (68 percent) there was no evidence of mental health contact in the correctional files. However, we did find that 7 percent had been subject to psychiatric evaluation, 8 percent were clients of substance abuse programs, 15 percent had been psychiatric patients, and 2 percent were treated for combined psychiatric and substance abuse problems. Thus, these data indicate that while our computerized matching procedure was an efficient screening device, the accuracy of identifying mental health clients was substantially increased by tapping more than one information source.

As a final step we used the composite service delivery information to reclassify the sample into three mental health groups—

substance abuse (n = 83), psychiatric (n = 540), and combined psychiatric and substance abuse (n = 141). Offenders with no history of mental health treatment, including those who were only subject to psychiatric evaluation, as well as the forensic clients for whom we were unable to verify service delivery, became the comparison group (n = 543).[11]

Before describing our analytic strategies, we must turn to issues that pertain to the generalizability of the sample. Specifically, we must consider how the results of this study can inform us about relationships between violence and emotional disorders and about other populations of mentally ill violent individuals.

Our sample derives from a group of violent offenders recently convicted and sentenced to prison. The criminal justice system is often likened to a sieve or filter in that at each successive juncture only some offenders continue in the process. We know that, among the factors that determine which offenders move forward, the most critical are offense seriousness and criminal history. Since ours is a prison intake sample, the violent individuals we studied have probably engaged in more serious violence and accumulated more extensive criminal records than other offenders not yet incarcerated.

Mentally disordered offenders are also identified on the basis of participation in outpatient and inpatient therapeutic programs. We know that not all persons with mental illness receive treatment, but among those who do we can be reasonably assured most are experiencing emotional difficulties. The process by which persons with emotional disorders seek assistance is influenced by the availability of formal and informal treatment options, which, in turn, depends on the level of social and economic resources. Inmates largely come from socially disadvantaged groups, and the disturbed individuals in our sample are probably unable to afford private caregivers, which means their emotional difficulties are more likely to be a matter of public record. We also

11. In the final classification, substance abusers are defined as persons who participated in either alcohol or drug treatment programs operating under psychiatric or nonpsychiatric auspices; psychiatric patients are defined as individuals who received outpatient or inpatient mental health treatment, exclusive of outpatient psychiatric evaluations.

know that the caseloads of public mental health institutions contain many of the seriously disordered individuals in our society.

Our criteria for defining substance abusers again refer to participation in treatment programs, and we know from reading inmate files that the definition does not include a fair number of offenders who habitually use drugs or who abuse alcohol. We assume that we have identified those with the most serious addiction problems, but we cannot be certain of this. However, many of our findings regarding these offenders (reported in chapters 3 and 5) are consistent with what is known about the relationship between substance abuse and crime.

The selectivity of our sampling procedures yields several advantages. By concentrating on the extremes of the crime spectrum we deal with serious violence, which is a major social problem, as well as with chronic offenders, a group that is of clear policy interest and that is likely to show substantial career patterns. In addition, by focusing on treated disturbed individuals, relationships between violence and emotional disorder should be easier to identify. We therefore are in a better position to raise treatment issues, including those pertaining to use of therapeutic alternatives to punitive responses.

Data Analysis

Our data analysis procedures can be divided into two major sections: (1) comparisons of offenders and violent incidents, and (2) development of a career typology describing histories of violent offense behavior and mental health involvement.

In making comparisons between offenders we focus on differences in criminal histories and mental health histories. We are especially interested in the frequency, nature, and timing of offense and mental-health-related involvements since this information becomes critical to us when we try to develop a typology that is largely based on history. Differences in social and demographic variables such as age, race, and marital status must also be examined.

Our comparison of violent incidents is based on the offense which has led to the offender's current term of imprisonment.

The information covers legal attributes such as statutory category and sentence length, as well as type of attack (for example, threat, physical assault), weapon use, location of incident, and the relationship of victim to offender. In collecting victim information we limited our coverage to two victims, giving priority to those who experienced the greatest injury. (This strategy did not prove too much of a limitation since only 15 percent of cases involved three or more victims.)

Unfortunately, legalistic descriptions may gloss over important commonalities between violent incidents; since statutory schemes are developed as punishment-relevant classifications, they do not always describe the uses to which violence is put. For example, an offender who attacks his or her spouse in a jealous rage might be convicted of either murder or assault depending on the postattack condition of the victim, which in turn can be influenced by such factors as celerity of medical attention. Legalistic schemes may draw our attention to a distinction in one area (for example, the victim's physical condition) at the expense of another (for example, the offender's motivation). In similar fashion, burglary, usually a nonviolent offense, can involve either threatened or actual violence against a confronted victim. We therefore developed a supplementary classification of violent incidents to describe the type and level of violence. The coding was based on offense descriptions provided by the prison system in the "description of pattern of criminal behavior" document, which is generated as part of the inmate classification process.

In describing types of violence we tried to keep our categorizations as close to the act as possible. We divided violent acts into unmotivated, retaliatory, felony-related, sex—adult, sex—child, weapon-related, arson, against police, burglary, auto, and institutional violence. Although we sometimes used legal designations of offenses (burglary, arson), at other times we restated statutory categories in broader terms (sex offenses, weapon offenses) or made victim-related distinctions not always reflected in the designations of conviction offenses (victims as adults, children, police). Where useful, we also incorporated motivational (unmotivated, retaliatory) or situational (felony-related, auto—as weapon/institution—as setting) elements to help describe violent behavior.

The distribution of conviction offenses by type of violence is shown in table 2.2. We see that some violence types (burglary, weapon offenses, and arson) are highly concordant with a specific offense, while other violence types (unmotivated, retaliatory, police victim, by auto or in institutions) contain a great deal of heterogeneity.

Since the violence type categories encompass substantial variation in levels of violence, we added a four-category ordinal scale to summarize the degree of harm inflicted on the victim. The categories used were no (personal) violence, less serious (threat or minor damage), serious (physical damage and nonconsensual sex), and extreme (death, serious multiple injury, or sex with violence). This format allows us to include nonviolent encounters that are statutorily defined as violent, as well as less predatory offenses that involve only a potential for violence or that result in minor physical harm. In combination, the coding formats provide a richer classification of incidents which describes both type and degree of violence.

Eccentric Aspects of Offense Behavior

We are obviously concerned with relationships between mental illness and violence and, in particular, with the ways that serious emotional problems can shape the expression of violence. In studying violent incidents, it struck us that some offenders, particularly offenders with a history of mental health involvement, do not come across as stereotypical criminals in that their offenses show peculiar, odd, or eccentric features. These attributes are neither reflected in legal classifications nor fully captured by our supplementary coding formats. We therefore developed a third code of unusual or eccentric offense attributes to capture peculiarities of violent behavior. There are many such attributes, but the general categories we used are ineffectual behavior, frenzied mental state, symptomatic behavior, no apparent motivation, and no memory of event.[12] Such impressions were systematically col-

12. The specific items that constitute the general categories of eccentricity are the following: ineffectual behavior—turned self in to police, failed to leave the scene of crime when given the opportunity, left behind personal identification or

Table 2.2. Percent distribution of conviction offense by type of violence

Conviction offense	Retaliatory (n=182)	Unmotivated (n=50)	Felony-related (n=559)	Sex–adult victim (n=76)	Sex–child victim (n=88)	Weapon (n=68)	Arson (n=29)	Police victim (n=28)	Burglary (n=199)	Auto/institution (n=29)
Murder	37%	25%	4%	1%	1%	2%	0%	0%	0%	0%
Kidnapping	1	0	0.7	3	0	0	0	0	0	0
Arson	0	0	0	0	0	0	97	0	0	0
Robbery	6	10	87	7	2	3	0	29	5	25
Assault	48	57	3	3	0	0	0	50	0.5	25
Reckless endangerment	4	2	0.2	0	0	0	0	4	0.5	0
Rape	0	0	0.2	64	43	0	0	4	0	0
Sodomy	0	0	0	13	38	0	0	0	0	0
Sex abuse	0	0	0	8	16	0	3	0	0	0
Weapon	3	4	0.7	1	0	91	0	7	1	4
Burglary	2	2	4	0	0	5	0	7	93	18

Note: Columns may not add to 100% because of rounding.

lected on the entire sample so as to allow for comparisons between the groups of offenders.

Career Framework

We have noted that any study of emotional disorders and violence
must accommodate the fact that mental health problems and
offense behaviors, and relationships between the two, change
over time. A concept that helps to organize this developmental
complexity is that of an offense–mental health "career." The
dictionary tells us that, apart from a sequence of vocational pro-
gression, a career can connote "a course of continued progress as
in the life of a person." Within the social sciences, a career frame-
work has been used to study a variety of progressions, including
the socialization of medical students, the development of drug
addiction, and the community adjustment of mental patients. In
these contexts, a career describes sequences of experiences that
are common to groups of individuals.

The goal of our research is to illuminate sequences of offender
behavior in which the advent of criminal acts and of symptoms
that are serious enough to justify diagnosis and treatment can be

---

other highly incriminating materials, made several attempts at the crime before
succeeding; frenzied mental state—violent overkill including multiple stabbing or
shooting, potentially fatal beating or assault, torture or mutilation; symptomatic
behavior—psychotic symptoms such as hallucinations or delusions, paranoia,
dazed, bewildered, confused, or disoriented mental state, poor personal hygiene,
depressed, withdrawn, or crying, and self-injury.

We collected data on several types of eccentric offense behavior that are not
reported. One category, behavior disproportionate to stimulus, was deleted because it appeared in over 50 percent of the cases and did not discriminate between
offender groups. In contrast, other eccentricity categories (matricide, fratricide,
or infanticide; excessive destruction of physical property) proved to be extremely
infrequent. Still other eccentric behavior (arson, sexual violence, child victim) is
better described by the type of violence codes we developed.

The category unmotivated offense appears in both the type of violence and
eccentric offense behavior classifications. The type of violence code describes the
primary nature of the violence and thus applies only to violent incidents. The
eccentricity code includes nonviolent and potentially violent encounters.

located in time. Such patterns of behavior over time permit us to show when a person is unambiguously disturbed, when he is engaging in crime, and when he is both. Given a large enough sample, temporal patterning permits the grouping of offenders into types that are characterized by different admixtures and sequences of offenses and symptomatology. Over a lifetime, such types describe composite careers of criminality and mental illness; over limited periods they describe composite career segments.

Career types are different chains of career segments which imply different relationships between personal problems and offense behavior. For example, offenses that are always committed when an offender has discontinued outpatient care and medication carry different implications from those that occur when the offender is receiving mental health services or when the offender has not yet been diagnosed. A career in which early emotional problems are followed by a long, rootless existence (unemployment, homelessness, and so forth) that eventually leads to criminality is different from a career of chronic delinquency and of incarceration followed by a psychotic breakdown.

Composite careers of criminality and mental disorder, reconstructed from chronologically based records, can help to illuminate patterns of escalation and deescalation or continuity and discontinuity of problem behaviors. One such example of a composite career, taken from the *New York Times*, describes the history of a man shot dead by police after running naked through St. Patrick's Cathedral in New York City and killing an elderly usher with a prayer stand.[13]

The account reads as follows:

June 23, 1983 First admitted to Bellevue Hospital Center. Was brought in for smashing windows of a Broadway movie theatre. Was under arrest in prison unit. Discharged July 1.

July 2 First incarcerated at Riker's island July 2, 1983, charged with third-degree assault. Released Aug. 8.

13. "A Killer in St. Patrick's: Hospital to Jail to Death," *New York Times*, September 23, 1988, pp. A1, B4.

Aug. 19 Bellevue. Was brought in after being found swimming in Hudson river. Discharged Sept. 7.

Sept. 10 Rikers. Charged with third-degree criminal trespassing. Released Oct. 11.

Feb. 9, 1984 Rikers. Charged with first-degree robbery. Released April 6.

April 16 Bellevue. Discharged April 23.

April 25 Bellevue. Discharged May 10.

Dec. 19 Bellevue. Examined in prison unit and released to police custody.

Dec. 20 Rikers. Charged with criminal possession of stolen property. Released Jan. 5, 1985.

Jan. 19, 1985 Rikers. Charged with petty larceny. Released Sept. 17.

Dec. 10 Bellevue. Discharged Jan. 6, 1986.

Feb. 27, 1986 Manhattan House of Detention. Charged with second-degree criminal trespassing. Released March 6.

Aug. 11, 1986 Rikers. Charged with fourth-degree criminal mischief. Released Sept. 19.

Sept. 25, 1986 Rikers. Charged with fourth-degree criminal mischief. Released Oct. 10.

March 26, 1987 Rikers. Charged with criminal mischief. Released April 10.

April 1 Bellevue. Treated in emergency room and given an appointment.

April 27 Bellevue. Seen for appointment.

April 28 Rikers. Charged with criminal mischief. Released May 8.

Sept. 23, 1988 Shot dead by police.

The career concept lends itself to the development of a career typology depicting common patterns of experience over time. As a descriptive tool, a career typology can be particularly useful because it organizes large amounts of data into meaningful and relevant subcategories. By including both offender and offense attributes in the same typology we can develop a composite picture of persons, histories, and behavior, and such combinations can provide clues to offense motivation as well as to other psychological processes associated with offending.

Various strategies can be used to develop a typological scheme. When relatively few items compose the dimensions of the typology, all possible or logical combinations can easily be examined. However, when the number of items involved is large this strategy becomes unwieldy, and a technique is needed to isolate significant combinations of variables.

A statistical procedure that is particularly well suited to the development of a discriminating classification scheme is cluster analysis. Cluster analysis refers to a family of statistical procedures used to identify groups or classes of objects with common attributes, the results of which can be viewed as a natural confluence taxonomy. The procedures can be applied to a variety of objects—people, institutions, cultures, plants, animals—and are especially useful with complicated data. For example, psychologists have used cluster techniques to identify patterns of personality characteristics among mentally ill and other individuals.[14] Thus, the analytic strategy is that of partitioning a diverse set of objects into clearly identified subsets based on regularly occurring linkages among items. Since one way we learn to organize experience is by sorting things on the basis of like and unlike features, cluster techniques have intuitive appeal because they are built around this familiar grouping strategy. Another attractive feature of cluster analysis is that by sorting a large heterogeneous group into smaller, more homogeneous subgroups, the technique can uncover otherwise hard-to-discern order and regularity in complex phenomena.

Applications of cluster procedures are considered atheoretical in the sense that hypotheses or theoretical propositions do not guide the statistical clustering process. However, there are several methodological issues that arise in the use of cluster analysis, and we will briefly outline these areas, documenting the strategies we employed to address them. The issues are (1) choosing variables for inclusion in the analysis, (2) selecting a clustering technique, (3) measuring similarity, and (4) deciding on the number of clusters in the final solution.

The selection of variables to be included in a cluster analysis is

14. Louis M. McQuitty, *Pattern-Analytic Clustering: Theory, Method, Research and Configural Findings* (New York: University Press of America, 1987).

important because there are limitless ways of describing objects and, by definition, omitted variables cannot be part of the taxonomy. We can therefore use our judgment to narrow the universe of descriptive items by eliminating those that seem conceptually irrelevant to the task at hand. Yet, after this step is taken, many options still exist, and choices can make a difference in producing a more or less meaningful classification scheme. Since we are concerned with offense–mental health careers, we had to include historical information on mental health and criminal justice experiences in our analysis. We also had to enter a description of the conviction offense which, given the procedures used to identify the sample, represents the capstone of the offender's violence career. The conviction offense was recorded in terms of type and level of violence, which we coded as described above. On the negative side we decided to exclude most demographic variables from the analysis because we felt that an initial focus on static background characteristics would prove distracting, particularly in the context of most other items which were chosen to illuminate sequences of pathology and violence.[15] We did, however, list demographic variables as "covariates" in our description of final cluster solutions.

The second issue with which we were confronted was that of selecting a clustering technique. A number of types of clustering techniques have been developed, and within a given type there are a variety of specific methods.[16] We decided to use a hierarchical technique which is appropriate for the types of data we collected and is among the more commonly used clustering procedures. Hierarchical techniques operate in an agglomerative manner, which means that at each step two groups are joined

15. We included age in the analysis since time, as it relates to opportunity (or in our case risk), is implicit in the notion of career, which describes developmental sequences.

16. Brian Everitt, *Cluster Analysis* (New York: John Wiley and Sons, 1974), 7–22. Among the more frequently used clustering techniques are hierarchical, optimization-partitioning, density or mode-seeking, and clumping. Hierarchical clustering methods include single linkage or nearest neighbor, complete linkage, or furthest neighbor, centroid, median, average linkage between or within groups, and Ward's method.

together, becoming a unit for subsequent mergers. In a figurative sense, the technique fashions a tree by starting with many individual branches and ending with a single trunk.[17] The specific clustering method we used is average linkage between groups, which tends to produce more homogeneous clusters than the single linkage method.[18]

The third issue involves the choice of a proximity measure to indicate degree of similarity or dissimilarity between objects. A problem researchers often face is that variables of different measurement levels are combined in an analysis, which means that selection of any single proximity measure involves compromise. In our situation, most of the variables in the analysis are nominal so that it was convenient to transform the data to binary (yes, no) format. We therefore generated dichotomous variables to represent the presence or absence of each of the nominal categories in the data set. In some cases it was necessary to reduce the level of measurement (as in the case of age) to accommodate this scheme.[19] After trying several proximity measures, we decided to use the Jaccard measure, which is one of several used with binary data.[20]

17. Michael Anderberg, *Cluster Analysis for Applications* (New York: Harcourt Brace Jovanovich, 1973), 131.

18. Average linkage is similar to single linkage, which is among the most popular clustering methods. However, average linkage is less influenced by extreme values and therefore less subject than single linkage to "chaining," which refers to the tendency for new clusters to be composed of a single case.

19. Age was divided into three categories: low (21 years and younger), medium (22 to 30 years), and high (31 years and older). Arrest history was similarly divided into the following categories: low (three or fewer arrests), medium (four to eight arrests) and high (nine or more arrests). Low IQ refers to test scores of 80 or less. Offenders with a history of psychotic diagnosis includes those who, at some time prior to entering the prison system, had received a clinical diagnosis (e.g., schizophrenia) involving psychotic symptoms (e.g., delusions, hallucinations). Offenders on probation or parole at the time of the offense are described as under supervision.

20. In a 2x2 table with frequencies a, b, c, d in respective cells (1,1) (1,0) (0,1) (0,0) the Jaccard measure is computed by $a/a+b+c$. Anderberg describes this measure as "the conditional probability that a randomly chosen data unit will score 1 on both variables, given that data units with 0-0 matches are discarded first. The 0-0 matches are treated as totally irrelevant" *Cluster Analysis for Applications*, 89.

The final issue is that of deciding on the number of clusters in the final solution. Hierarchical techniques generate from one to as many clusters as there are data points, and it is up to the researcher to decide where in the process to draw the line. Mechanical strategies have been developed to address this issue, but these methods are concerned with finding the "correct" number of clusters, a notion that is often of questionable relevance to hierarchical techniques. The conceptual "meaning" or "coherence" of items that defines the clusters was to us the important consideration, and we used this criterion in assessing various solutions. The point at which the disaggregation process no longer made useful or meaningful distinctions (or conversely, when the agglomeration process obscured useful distinctions) is the juncture that we identified as the final cluster solution.

Chapter 3

Results of
Statistical Analyses

In this chapter we examine the social, criminal, and mental health background of inmates in our sample. This review serves several purposes. First, it is a descriptive device, providing contextual material that allows for comparisons with other offender populations. The review also provides a frame of reference for subsequent analyses in that some findings may highlight areas for investigation, and others may facilitate explanations of results. In addition, by scrutinizing the criminal history of mental patients we broach the question that motivated our study, which is, What are the relationships between emotional disorder and violence? And, finally, by mapping the nature and timing of criminal and mental health involvements, we create a foundation for the career typology we shall describe in subsequent chapters.

Herein are included detailed comparisons of violent incidents by emotionally disordered and other offenders; this representation is directly relevant to our main concerns, which center on the distinctive features of violence among offenders with emotional problems. Our approach to the analysis will be twofold in that we shall include legal classifications and conventional offense attributes such as victim–offender relationship as descriptive items, in addition to comparisons based on the violence typology and the eccentricity codes we have described in chapter 2.

Social Characteristics and Criminal History

In table 3.1 we display the social characteristics and criminal histories of offenders in the samples. We find that in all three mental health groups white, nonhispanic inmates are overrepresented, with the highest percentage found among offenders with combined substance abuse and mental health problems (57 percent). We also note that inmates with a history of psychiatric problems show the lowest level of preincarceration employment and are least likely to be married. Finally, we see that inmates in the mental health groups tend to be older than other inmates, with the greatest difference found among the two groups of substance abusers. These findings are consistent with other research which has suggested that mentally disordered offenders tend to have less solid roots in the community than other offenders.[1]

We observe that violent offenders in our samples have accumulated substantial criminal records, with an average of 5.7 arrests for the comparison group. Yet offenders with mental health records have more extensive criminal backgrounds than other offenders, and this tendency includes a greater number of violent offenses. The difference is greatest among substance abusers, who on the average have almost twice as many arrests as offenders in the comparison group, making it unsurprising that inmates with substance abuse problems are more apt to have done time in prison. First contact with the criminal justice system occurs on the average at about eighteen years of age for all inmate groups, which means that differences in criminal histories cannot be attributed to earlier onset of offender careers. Another possible explanation for the differences in arrest histories is that they are an artifact of age disparities, given that older offenders have had more time to accumulate contacts with the criminal justice system. Yet when we group offenders into relatively homogeneous

1. When Steadman and his associates compared demographic profiles between hospital patients who are arrested and other patients, differences suggested patient-arrestees resembled offender populations (i.e., young, minority group members with prior criminal records) (Steadman et al., "Explaining the increased arrest rate"). On the other side of the coin we find that offenders with mental health backgrounds demographically resemble client populations of psychiatric hospitals (i.e., older, white individuals).

Table 3.1. Social characteristics and criminal history by mental health experience of offender

	No history (n=544)	Substance abuse history (n=83)	Psychiatric history (n=540)	Substance abuse and psychiatric history (n=141)
Social characteristics				
Ethnicity				
White	15%**	44%**	39%**	57%**
Black	58	34	46	30
Hispanic	27	22	15	13
Gender				
Male	98%	96%	96%	96%
Female	2	4	4	4
Marital status				
Single	64%**	65%**	77%**	71%**
Married	36	35	23	29
Highest education level				
Grade school	22%	20%	22%	19%
Some high school	64	61	56	59
High school graduate	16	19	21	23
Age (years at prison entry)	$\bar{x}$=26.0[a] sd= 7.7	$\bar{x}$=30.4[a] sd= 6.6	$\bar{x}$=28.6[a] sd= 9.4	$\bar{x}$=30.0[a] sd= 7.6
Employed (at conviction)	78%**	82%**	69%**	85%**
Criminal history				
Age at first offense (years)[b]	$\bar{x}$=18.4 sd= 6.1	$\bar{x}$=17.6 sd= 2.8	$\bar{x}$=18.4 sd= 8.0	$\bar{x}$=17.8 sd= 4.4
Number of prior offenses	$\bar{x}$= 5.7[a] sd= 5.7	$\bar{x}$=10.0[a] sd= 7.1	$\bar{x}$= 7.9[a] sd= 7.5	$\bar{x}$=10.3[a] sd= 7.5
Number of prior violent offenses	$\bar{x}$= 1.4 sd= 1.7	$\bar{x}$= 1.9 sd= 2.4	$\bar{x}$= 1.8 sd= 2.2	$\bar{x}$= 2.0 sd= 2.2
Prior prison experience	27%**	43%**	31%**	48%**

**Chi-square, p. less than .01

[a]T-test, p. less than .01

[b]The conviction offense is used as the first offense for offenders with no criminal history.

age strata,[2] we find comparable differences in arrest histories by mental health background, showing that offenders with emotional problems have greater levels of criminal involvement irrespective of chronological age.

Patterns of Prior Offenses

The number of prior violent crimes committed by an individual is strongly associated with the number of nonviolent crimes (Pearson correlation = .62). This finding confirms that criminals lead checkered offense careers, and raises the possibility that more extensive violence histories among offenders with mental health problems may simply reflect a more general increased propensity to crime. One strategy for addressing this issue is to examine the percent distribution of prior offenses by type, which provides an index of crime propensity that in effect is standardized for number of offenses. These data are shown in table 3.2, and our discussion will focus on ratios across groups of offenders within types of crime.

We see that the comparison group of offenders is about one and a half times more likely to have been arrested for robbery

2. Mean arrest rates across age categories and offender groups (1 - comparison, 2 - substance abuse, 3 - psychiatric, 4 - combined substance abuse-psychiatric) are as follows:

Mean number of prior arrests

	Offender group			
Age at conviction offense	*1*	*2*	*3*	*4*
20 years and younger	3.4	4.1	5.0	4.6
21 to 25 years	5.3	7.1	7.0	7.9
26 to 30 years	6.6	9.1	9.5	11.1
31 to 35 years	8.0	10.0	10.0	10.4
36 to 40 years	8.9	17.1	8.6	10.9
41 years and older	8.5	15.4	9.5	20.5

The data indicate that offenders with mental health backgrounds have more extensive criminal histories than other offenders across age groups. The difference is greatest for offenders with substance abuse problems, especially in the older age groups, where we find very substantial criminal records.

Table 3.2. Distribution of types of prior offenses by mental health experience of offender

	No history (n, offenses =3,067)	Substance abuse history (n=810)	Psychiatric history (n=4,179)	Substance abuse and psychiatric history (n=1,429)
Type of prior offenses				
Murder	0.5%	0.4%	0.3%	0.4%
Kidnapping	0.1	0.2	0.2	0.3
Arson	0.5	0.6	0.4	0.5
Rape, sodomy, sex abuse	1.5	1.6	2.7	1.6
Robbery	14.0	9.4	8.9	9.1
Assault	6.7	5.6	9.5	6.9
Reckless endangerment	1.2	1.7	1.8	1.8
Burglary	14.3	17.7	14.4	16.9
Grand larceny	11.6	10.6	9.4	8.5
Possess stolen property	5.6	4.9	4.3	4.2
Petit larceny	8.3	8.4	9.2	10.6
Forgery, fraud	2.9	3.1	4.6	4.3
Prostitution	0.2	3.1	0.9	0.3
Drug	6.6	8.1	4.2	6.4
Marijuana	4.5	3.3	1.9	2.7
Firearm	4.0	3.1	2.9	2.4
Public order	3.2	5.1	6.1	5.3
Criminal mischief	2.1	2.7	3.8	2.4
Criminal trespass	3.9	2.3	3.9	3.3
Harassment	1.2	1.1	2.0	1.8
Escape	0.4	0.7	0.6	1.0
Resisting arrest	1.5	1.4	1.1	1.4
Gambling	0.7	0.5	0.8	0.1
DWI	0.7	2.5	1.3	2.2
Other auto	1.1	1.2	1.5	1.9
Juvenile delinquency	1.8	0.5	1.5	2.7
Person in need of supervision	1.0	0.1	2.1	0.7

than other offenders. In contrast, those in the three mental health groups are twice as likely to have been arrested for public order offenses. Both groups of substance abusers reveal an inclination for burglary and drug offenses and substantially stand out from the comparison group by being about three times more likely to have been arrested for driving while intoxicated (DWI). Offenders with relatively pure substance abuse problems are also about fifteen times more likely to have been arrested for prostitution. Finally, we find that the psychiatric group is about one and a half times more likely than the comparison group to have been arrested for assault, including sexual assaults such as rape and sodomy, as well as for criminal mischief.[3]

In summary, the data indicate that offenders with mental health histories, particularly substance abuse problems, have much more extensive criminal records than other offenders. Among the more significant findings is the fact that offenders with psychiatric histories show a greater propensity for assaultive offenses, including serious sexual assaults. Substance abusers are more frequently involved with possessing or selling drugs and DWI. They also show a greater inclination for burglary and prostitution offenses, activities which presumably can help finance addictions. At the same time, all groups of offenders with mental health involvements show a disproportionate tendency for nuisance offenses, such as those considered breaches of public order.

The greater propensity that offenders with mental health histories have for both violent and nuisance offenses is somewhat

3. In order to investigate if serious offenders with mental health backgrounds have a tendency to specialize in violence we examined the proportion of violent to total crimes among offenders with ten or more prior arrests. The analysis revealed that the distribution of this proportion was virtually identical across offender groups. Descriptive statistics on the distributions are as follows:

	Mean	Standard deviation	Median
Comparison group	.22	.15	.19
Substance abuse group	.20	.16	.16
Psychiatric group	.23	.18	.19
Combined substance abuse and psychiatric group	.20	.16	.17

paradoxical, given that our image of disturbed violent offenders is different from that of the town drunk who panhandles and sleeps on park benches, or from that of the mental patient who wanders the street determined to engage pedestrians in strangely symbolic conversations. This observation led us to ask the question whether the two tendencies coexist in the same individual or characterize nonoverlapping subgroups of offenders, and we pursued the issue by looking at the association between numbers of violent and public order offenses. The analysis revealed substantial Pearson correlations among substance abusers (.24) and among offenders with composite psychiatric–substance abuse problems (.37), and considerably lower correlations among offenders with a psychiatric history (.15) or with no record of mental health involvement (.13).

Our findings pointed to a connection between substance abuse problems and the kinds of crimes offenders commit, and we suspected that these relationships were obscured by the mix of alcoholics and drug addicts in the substance abuse groups. We therefore looked at criminal histories by type of addiction and found that alcoholics had a greater propensity to engage in arson, assault, reckless endangerment, public order offenses, and DWI (see table in note 4 below). In contrast, drug addicts were disproportionately involved in burglary and drug offenses, including marijuana offenses. These findings help confirm the argument that drug addicts can be financially motivated to commit property offenses in support of their addiction, and that one consequence of laws designed to curb the use of drugs is that of turning addicts into repeat offenders.

Contrasting criminal proclivities, such as engaging in social nuisance and violent offenses, were shown to have a greater tendency to appear in tandem among substance abusers. This finding requires us to bring a new perspective to the fact that offenders with alcohol problems disproportionately engage in a variety of antisocial behavior ranging in degree of seriousness from public order offenses to arson. It not only appears that portraits of alcoholics as disorderly drunks and as bellicose inebriates both contain an element of truth, but, more significant, we find that these representations often describe coexisting dispositions in the same intoxicated person. Also, we note that the violence pattern (arson, assault, reckless endangerment) among alcoholics points to a phenomenon that reinforces another familiar argument, that of postulating a link between severe drinking, emotional disinhibition, and impaired social judgment.[4]

Offender Career Patterns

We now examine mental health and criminal justice careers based on the chronology of treatment involvements and arrests for

4. The distribution of types of prior offenses by type of substance abuse problem is as follows:

	Alcohol (n = 698)	Drug (n = 1,229)	Both (n = 312)
Murder	0.4%	0.4%	0.3%
Kidnapping	0.4	0.2	0
Arson	1.1	0.2	0.6
Rape, sodomy, sex abuse	1.7	1.5	1.9
Robbery	9.6	9.1	8.7
Assault	8.3	6.0	3.8
Reckless endangerment	2.9	1.0	2.6
Burglary	13.6	18.6	19.9
Grand larceny	9.3	9.6	8.0
Possess stolen property	3.3	5.0	4.8
Petty larceny	8.9	10.4	9.6
Forgery or fraud	5.0	3.7	1.9
Prostitution	0.3	1.2	3.2
Drug offenses	2.4	9.8	6.4
Marijuana offenses	0.9	4.1	3.2
Firearm offenses	2.1	2.8	2.9
Public order	9.6	2.8	4.8
Criminal mischief	3.4	1.5	4.5
Criminal trespass	2.7	3.1	2.9
Harassment	3.2	0.9	0.6
Escape	0.6	1.3	0.3
Resisting arrest	1.9	1.0	1.9
Gambling	0	0.3	0.3
DWI	4.9	1.1	1.3
Other auto offenses	1.6	1.5	2.6
Juvenile delinquency	1.6	2.0	1.9
Person in need of supervision	0.3	0.5	1.0

violence.[5] In order to simplify the analysis, we have characterized past events as remote (more than three years) or recent (three years or less). This scheme allows us to trace the recency and chronicity of criminal violence and of indications of mental disorder. We also identify instances of mental health treatment in connection with the violent conviction offense that defines the sample.

Patterns of mental health contacts over time are displayed in table 3.3. We note that more than half (56.3 percent) the substance abusers have a treatment history confined to the remote past, while other disordered offenders tend to show signs of having more current problems. If we tally offenders who have had mental health treatment within three years of the violent conviction offense, (that is, combine all patterns except remote past only) we find that three-fifths (60.7 percent) of the psychiatric group and seven-tenths (70.3 percent) of the combined psychiatric–substance abuse group demonstrate near-term evidence of emotional difficulties. In addition, we note that offenders with substance abuse and psychiatric disorders are most apt to have earned a client status that spans both remote and recent past (42.6 percent).

If we tally offenders in the psychiatric history group who re-

5. Information regarding the timing of service delivery was not always available for mental health contacts recorded in correctional files. The fact that the degree of completeness of treatment chronologies varied a great deal presented us with a problem. If we limited our analyses to individuals for whom we had complete information on all contacts, a substantial number of cases would be excluded as missing data. On the other hand, if we analyzed only events with complete information, descriptions of many individual mental health careers would be incomplete. We resolved the dilemma by assigning mental health contacts to the remote history category when the year of contact was unknown. We chose this strategy because, among events with complete information, a disproportionate number occurred more than three years prior to the conviction offense. Although this procedure introduces a bias that leads us to overestimate the frequency of remote mental health involvements, the error is less than if we listed events with missing dates in one of the other time categories. We also assigned June 30 as the date if only the year of contact was available, and we used the fifteenth of the month if only the day was missing. Finally, we included psychiatric evaluations at time of conviction in the career chronology, although these evaluations were not used in the initial classification of the mental health samples.

Table 3.3. Career patterns of treatment history by mental health experience of offender

Chronology of treatment	Substance abuse history (n=80)	Psychiatric history (n=537)	Substance abuse and psychiatric history (n=191)
Remote history only	56.3%	39.3%	29.8%
Remote and other history	20.1	37.6	57.5
Other history only	23.6	23.1	12.7
	100.0	100.0	100.0
Recent history only	18.8%	8.8%	5.0%
Recent and other history	15.1	30.1	53.3
Other history only	66.1	61.1	41.7
	100.0	100.0	100.0
At conviction only	3.8%	8.8%	3.5%
At conviction and other history	8.9	30.5	19.2
Other history only	87.3	60.7	77.3
	100.0	100.0	100.0
Combination patterns:			
Remote and recent	12.5%	12.7%	42.6%
Remote and at conviction	6.3	13.2	8.5
Recent and at conviction	1.3	5.6	4.3
Remote, recent, and at conviction	1.3	11.7	6.4
Subtotal:	21.4%	43.2%	61.8%
Simple patterns:	78.6%	56.8%	38.2%
	100.0	100.0	100.0

Note: Remote history refers to events taking place more than three years prior to the conviction offense, and recent history refers to events within three years of the conviction offense.

ceived services at conviction, we find that the proportion is substantial (39.3 percent). However, treatment histories limited to this point in time are in the minority (8.8 percent of the group), since most offenders who received services at conviction have a record of previous mental health involvement. A similar though less substantial pattern holds for psychiatric patients with substance abuse problems.

If we define chronic histories as those with treatment involvements spanning the three time periods, we find that substance abusers show the least chronicity and psychiatric patients the most. In particular, we see that about one in nine (11.7 percent) of the purely psychiatric patients can be described as a chronic mental health client.

In table 3.4 we display chronological patterns of violence. In this table, we confirm that the comparison group has the highest proportion of offenders with no violence history (38.6 percent), while the combined substance abuse and psychiatric group has the lowest proportion (22.7 percent). Whereas both substance abuse groups tend to have violence histories limited to the remote past (44.6 percent and 51.1 percent), all mental health groups show greater chronicity of violence than the comparison group, with the psychiatric group being the most chronic (18.9 percent). Although the differences in the proportion of chronic violent offenders are not dramatic, for nearly one in five offenders with a mental health history the offense for which he or she was incarcerated represents at minimum his or her third arrest for a violent crime.

Next we examined the relationship between temporal patterns of mental health contacts and violence, and the results of this analysis are shown in table 3.5. A remote violence history appears most characteristic of substance abusers, regardless of treatment chronology, and chronic substance abusers contain the largest proportion of chronically violent offenders (29.4 percent).

Both groups of psychiatric patients, those with relatively pure emotional problems and those with additional substance abuse problems, display similar relationships between chronologies of treatment and violence. Offenders with a remote treatment history most often have a violence history limited to the same early time frame (42.2 percent and 57.1 percent), but half or more of those who only recently became mental health clients have no violence history (50.0 percent and 52.1 percent). Chronic psychiatric patients show nearly equal proportions of offenders with no violence history (31.9 percent) or a history of remote violence (31.0 percent), whereas those with additional substance abuse problems more often than not have a remote violence history (51.7 percent). Finally, both groups of chronic psychiatric pa-

Table 3.4. Career patterns of violence history by mental health experience of offender

| | Mental health experience | | | |
Violence history	No history (n=544)	Substance abuse history (n=83)	Psychiatric history (n=540)	Substance abuse and psychiatric history (n=141)
No prior violence	38.6%	27.7%	34.1%	22.7%
Remote violence	30.9	44.6	32.4	51.1
Recent violence	16.7	9.6	14.6	9.2
Recent and remote violence	13.8	18.1	18.9	17.0

Note: Remote history refers to events taking place more than three years prior to the conviction offense, and recent history refers to events within three years of the conviction offense.

tients contain a substantial proportion of chronically violent offenders (20.7 percent and 19.5 percent).

Overall, we find that many offenders who have been psychiatric patients have long-standing treatment histories. More significant, we see that violent offenders who raise mental health issues at conviction usually have a prior record of emotional difficulty. In contrast, treatment chronologies of substance abusers tend to be more circumscribed, less often spanning remote and recent past. Substance abusers, who also tend to be the oldest offenders in our samples, also have violence careers that are limited to the remote past, while other offenders more often have a history of recent violence. Careers of violence show somewhat greater chronicity among offenders with records of mental health problems, and this finding is consistent with our previous analyses.

The relationship between mental health and violence careers is reported in table 3.5, where we see a consistent and significant pattern among both groups of former psychiatric patients. Offenders with a history of psychiatric treatment originating long in the past usually have a violence history confined to the same time

Table 3.5. Relationship between treatment career patterns and violence career patterns by type of mental health history

		Violence history			
	Treatment history	*No violence*	*Remote violence*	*Recent violence*	*Remote and recent violence*
Offenders with a	Remote (n=45)	26.7%	44.4%	11.1%	17.8%
Substance Abuse	Recent (n=18)	33.3	50.0	11.1	5.6
History	Remote and recent (n=15)	23.5	41.2	5.9	29.4
Offenders with a	Remote (n=211)	28.4	42.2	10.9	18.5
Psychiatric	Recent (n=94)	52.1	13.8	19.1	14.9
History	Remote and recent (n=232)	31.9	31.0	16.4	20.7
Offenders with a	Remote (n=42)	23.8	57.1	7.1	11.9
Substance Abuse	Recent (n=12)	50.0	25.0	8.3	16.7
and Psychiatric	Remote and				
History	recent (n=87)	18.4	51.7	10.3	19.5

Note: In this table, recent treatment history includes services delivered after the conviction offense.

frame. Similarly, convicted violent offenders who have only recently developed emotional difficulties tend to have no prior record of violence and are often first-time violent offenders, and psychiatric patients with chronic treatment histories are most likely to have chronic violence histories. Thus, as we track the course of mental health treatments over time, periods of serious emotional disorder consistently coincide with an increased propensity to violence. The pattern is significant because it suggests a connection between emotional problems and violence among seriously disturbed offenders.

Offense Descriptions

In table 3.6 we describe the offenses for which inmates in the samples were incarcerated. The data indicate that offenders with

Table 3.6. Conviction offense and sentence length by mental health experience of offender

| | Mental health experience | | | | Mean sentence length[a] (Months) | | | | | | | |
	No history (n=544)	Substance abuse history (n=83)	Psychiatric history (n=540)	Substance abuse and psychiatric history (n=141)	Min	Max	Min	Max	Min	Max	Min	Max
Conviction offense												
Murder	8.8%	6.0%	10.4%	5.7%	56	163	42	107	67	182	61	153
Kidnapping	0.2	0.0	0.9	0.7	b	b	b	b	46	108	b	b
Arson	1.1	2.4	3.0	2.8	20	50	b	b	28	73	b	b
Robbery	46.6	44.6	32.4	44.7	37	85	43	84	37	82	42	94
Assault	9.4	7.2	16.1	12.1	38	80	39	87	39	86	30	71
Reckless endangerment	0.4	1.2	1.1	1.4	b	b	b	b	27	61	b	b
Burglary	15.8	24.1	16.1	21.3	31	72	32	72	32	71	33	72
Rape	5.2	4.8	9.3	3.5	55	140	b	b	55	125	54	130
Sodomy	2.0	2.4	5.7	0.0	32	88	b	b	39	103	b	b
Sex abuse	1.1	2.4	2.4	0.0	16	48	b	b	16	49	b	b
Weapon	9.4	4.8	2.6	7.8	28	50	b	b	32	67	21	47

[a]Offenders with a life sentence are excluded from the table.
[b]Statistic not reported because there are fewer than five cases.

psychiatric histories more often stand convicted of murder, assault, rape, and sodomy, implying that the degree of physical injury inflicted on victims is highest for this group. On the other hand, offenders in both substance abuse groups are more apt to stand convicted of burglary, which suggests that these groups did the least physical damage to victims.

In the same table we see that psychiatric patients convicted of murder, arson, rape, and weapon offenses received longer sentences than others similarly convicted. In contrast, inmates with combined substance abuse and psychiatric problems were at risk for relatively longer sentences if convicted of robbery or assault, and for shorter sentences if convicted of weapon possession. Finally, offenders with substance abuse problems convicted of murder appear to have been sentenced to a shorter term of incarceration in comparison with other murderers.

In addition to the items shown in table 3.6, we examined the proportion of offenders under community supervision at the time of the offense, convicted by trial, and sentenced to life imprisonment. The analysis did not reveal any significant differences across groups of inmates.

In summary, we find inmates with psychiatric histories more often sentenced for serious violent crimes and substance abusers more frequently incarcerated for burglary. Differences in conviction offenses thus parallel differences observed in arrest histories, and this confluence of findings is reassuring because it suggests that there are reliable differences in criminal propensity between groups of offenders. The fact that similar differences emerge across both arrest histories and conviction offenses also points to some continuity in offense behavior over time. Finally, although we have not examined a number of factors that enter into sentencing decisions, the data support the argument that mentally disordered offenders receive more severe penalties than other offenders similarly convicted, especially when sentenced for very serious violent crimes.

Patterns of Offense Behavior

At this point we describe aspects of violent crimes (for example, location, weapon use, victim–offender relationship) often reported in criminological research. In so doing, we locate violent offenses by disturbed offenders within a broad context of situational attributes. As we reviewed these data, we noticed that a modal, or typical, pattern, around which there is modest variation, existed for each crime type. We therefore start to report the findings with a composite description of "typical" offense by the comparison group and then note any deviations from this pattern by offenders in the mental health groups. In table 3.7 we present information on selected characteristics of violent crimes by the offender's mental health experience.

Murderers commit most of their offenses on the street or at the victim's residence, using a gun, and are often accompanied by a cooffender. The victim is typically a male friend or acquaintance. In contrast, murderers with psychiatric histories are more likely to act alone at their own residences, using a blunt instrument as weapon, killing a relative or spouse.

Murders and assaults share a similar pattern of offense characteristics. Among the comparison group, assaults tend to occur on the street against a male friend or acquaintance. The incidents frequently involve a gun, and the victim usually requires hospital treatment. Offenders with psychiatric histories prefer to act alone in off-the-street locations, assaulting female strangers. They rarely use a weapon, but when they do, the preferred instrument is a knife, and the attack is less likely to precipitate hospitalization. Inmates with combined psychiatric and substance abuse histories disproportionately attack their relatives or spouse and, when a weapon is used, more often than not it is a knife.

Robbers constitute the largest offender group, and the typical scenario finds the offender on the street acting in concert with others and with a weapon, usually a gun. The victim is nearly always a stranger and suffers physical assault. Several contrasts with this picture are found among the substance abusers. Both groups (specialized, compounded) of substance abusers tend to commit their robberies without assistance against commercial establishments. The victim is usually threatened with a weapon, and the offender makes off with a substantial amount of money (over $250).

Sex offenders almost always act alone, committing the offense at their or the victim's domicile with a relatively young (under 16 years of age) female victim who is either a friend or stranger.

Table 3.7. Selected characteristics of violent incidents by type of offense and mental health experience of offender

	Mental health experience			
	No history	Substance abuse	Psychiatric history	Substance abuse and psychiatric history
Murder	*(n=48)*	*(n=5)*	*(n=56)*	*(n=8)*
2 or more offenders	37.5%*	20.0%*	16.1%*	50.0%*
Location				
Residence	34.0%	40.0%	48.2%	50.0%
Business	19.1	20.0	14.3	0.0
Street	42.6	40.0	33.9	37.5
Other	4.3	0.0	3.6	12.5
Weapon				
None	0.0%	20.0%	5.4%	0.0%
Knife	33.3	40.0	39.3	50.0
Gun	56.3	40.0	30.4	37.5
Blunt instrument	2.1	0.0	14.3	0.0
Other	8.4	0.0	10.7	12.5
Victim's relationship to offender				
Spouse, paramour	12.5%	20.0%	17.9%	12.5%
Other relative	0.0	0.0	3.6	0.0
Friend, acquaintance	52.2	40.0	50.0	62.5
Stranger	34.8	40.0	28.6	25.0
Male victim	75.0%	60.0%	76.8%	75.0%
Assault	*(n=51)*	*(n=6)*	*(n=87)*	*(n=17)*
Two or more offenders	23.5%	0.0%	14.9%	0.0%
Location				
Offender's residence	15.7%	16.7%	17.4%	37.5%
Victim's residence	15.7	16.7	14.0	12.5
Business	11.8	0.0	12.8	18.8
Street	47.1	50.0	38.4	25.0
Other	9.8	16.7	17.4	6.3
Weapon				
None	7.8%	33.3%	14.9%	11.8%

Table 3.7 Continued

	Mental health experience			
	No history	Substance abuse	Psychiatric history	Substance abuse and psychiatric history
Knife	31.4*	50.0*	51.7*	64.7*
Gun	49.0**	16.7**	18.4**	11.8**
Other	11.8	0.0	14.9	11.8
Victim's relationship to offender				
Spouse, paramour	14.0%	16.7%	19.5%	29.4%
Other relative	2.0	0.0	1.1	11.8
Friend, acquaintance	54.0	33.3	35.4	41.2
Police	5.9	16.7	9.8	5.9
Stranger	28.0	33.3	40.2	17.6
Victim hospitalized	70.6%	50.0%	48.8%	47.1%
Female victim	27.5%	50.0%	42.5%	41.2%
Robbery	(n=253)	(n=37)	(n=175)	(n=63)
Two or more offenders	70.8%**	54.1%**	47.4%**	34.9%**
Over $250	23.4	35.5	26.8	37.5
Location				
Victim's residence	13.5%	10.8%	16.7%	17.5%
Business	20.7**	40.5**	26.4**	49.2**
Public transportation	14.7	5.4	14.4	11.1
Street	47.4**	43.2**	38.5**	17.5**
Other	3.6	0.0	4.0	4.8
Weapon				
None	29.8%	16.2%	31.8%	19.7%
Knife	23.0	37.8	27.2	29.5
Gun	43.7	43.2	35.3	47.5
Other	3.6	2.7	5.7	3.2
Stranger victim	84.5%	97.3%	83.4%	81.0%
Most serious attack				
Threatened	35.3%**	64.9%**	35.6%**	61.9%**

Table 3.7 *Continued*

	Mental health experience			
	No history	*Substance abuse*	*Psychiatric history*	*Substance abuse and psychiatric history*
Hit, hand or object	53.8**	29.7**	54.6**	33.3**
Shot or stabbed	10.4	5.4	8.6	4.8
Raped	0.4	0.0	1.1	0.0
Sex offense	*(n=48)*	*(n=8)*	*(n=94)*	*(n=5)*
Two or more offenders	8.9%	0.0%	7.4%	20.0%
Location				
Offender's residence	40.0%	37.5%	42.2%	20.0%
Victim's residence	26.7	25.0	27.8	0.0
Street	17.8	37.5	15.6	40.0
Other	15.6	0.0	14.4	40.0
Weapon used	28.9%	12.5%	24.7%	40.0%
Male victim	11.1%	25.0%	22.3%	0.0%
Victim under 16	55.6%	50.0%	58.5%	20.0%
Victim's relationship to offender				
Spouse, paramour	4.5%	0.0%	4.3%	20.0%
Daughter, son	13.6	37.5	14.3	0.0
Other relative	0.0	0.0	5.5	0.0
Friend, acquaintance	45.4	37.5	39.6	40.0
Stranger	36.4	25.0	38.5	40.0
Weapon	*(n=51)*	*(n=4)*	*(n=14)*	*(n=11)*
Two or more offenders	25.5%	25.0%	21.4%	36.4%
Location				
Residence	23.5%	25.0%	21.4%	0.0%
Business	5.9	25.0	21.4	27.3
Public transportation	5.9	0.0	7.1	9.1
Street	64.7	50.0	50.0	63.6
Victim physically attacked	7.8%	25.0%	21.4%	9.1%

Table 3.7 *Continued*

	Mental health experience			
	No history	*Substance abuse*	*Psychiatric history*	*Substance abuse and psychiatric history*
Burglary	*(n=86)*	*(n=20)*	*(n=82)*	*(n=30)*
Two or more offenders	48.8%	30.0%	35.6%	23.3%
Over $250	45.3%	41.2%	50.7%	47.4%
Location				
Residence	88.4%	85.0%	92.0%	96.7%
Business	9.3	10.0	4.6	3.3
Other	2.3	5.0	3.4	0.0

*p. less than .05; **p. less than .01; Chi-square, specified category versus all others.

Note: The chi-square test statistic is strongly influenced by the number of cases, which for some offender and offense combinations is very small. Percentages refer to the proportion of incidents with a given characteristic. Some columns may sum to greater than 100% because multiple victims with different characteristics are involved. The number of cases may vary as a result of missing data. Descriptive items are reported selectively since all items are not relevant to each offense type. Infrequently appearing categories are sometimes combined. The offender's residence is counted as the offense location in situations where offender and victim live together.

Weapons are infrequently used. The mental health groups show the same pattern, with the exception of the psychiatric group, which is somewhat more likely to search out a male victim.

Burglars, acting in concert, usually target the private dwelling of a stranger. The crime often produces substantial material gain (over $250), and victims are rarely physically assaulted. A similar pattern emerges for mental health groups, except that these offenders show a greater propensity to act alone.

Weapons offenses often involve a lone offender who is discovered carrying a weapon on the street. Only in rare instances is there a victim who is attacked. A similar pattern is found among the mental health groups. However, incidents by offenders with psychiatric histories appear to carry a greater potential for violence, as indicated by a greater tendency to be found carrying weapons in commercial establishments and attacking a victim.

In summary, the composite picture that describes many, but certainly not all, murders and assaults among the comparison group is as follows: The violence is a product of street encounters among groups of male acquaintances in which a dispute arises and someone is shot. Major departures from this scenario for offenders with mental health histories, particularly psychiatric care, are: (1) the offender is more inclined to act alone, (2) incidents are less likely to take place on the streets, (3) the offender less often uses a gun, (4) murders more frequently involve non-stranger victims, specifically a spouse or relative, and (5) strangers and females show greater chances of being victims of assault.

Before discussing our findings we need to acknowledge that several explanations can be applied to the same set of facts. This is so because differences in criminal behavior may reflect variations in social activities or life styles of offenders, or may capture different motivational or situational aspects of violent encounters. At a later point we will examine violent incidents from a different perspective, one that will provide additional information on these issues. Nevertheless, we now venture a few interpretations of the data we have just presented.

The most consistent difference we find, one that applies to almost all types of crime, is that offenders with mental health backgrounds are more disposed to act alone. This fact suggests that group-influenced motivations are less apt to produce violence among mentally disordered offenders, which may reflect the familiar observation that mental patients tend to have relatively marginal life styles that include a greater degree of social isolation. The fact that mental patients use guns less often than other violent offenders suggests that disturbed offenders are less prone to share the view that possessing a gun is a necessary means of protection or a visible symbol of toughness. More generally, however, access to firearms depends upon associations with persons who have access to illegal goods and markets, and in this regard mental patients may be at a disadvantage.

Relatives and spouses are disproportionately victims of murder, implicating domestic problems as situations that can provoke extremely violent reactions from mentally disordered offenders.[6] We also find that violence by mental patients occurs less frequently on the streets, reinforcing the conclusion that different types of social situations or encounters act as a catalyst to violence. One possibility is that intimate family encounters are a source of stress for emotionally disordered persons and may, over time, lead to an escalation of accumulated grievances (including legitimate, exaggerated, or imagined grievances). Yet, intimates will probably also be exposed to greater risk of victimization because disturbed offenders lead more reclusive lives.

In contrast, assault victims are more often strangers, which suggests that unprovoked attacks or short-term escalations of ordinary social encounters may be more prevalent among mentally disordered offenders. It is harder to explain why females are more frequently chosen as victims, but it may be that some disturbed offenders lack inhibitions including chivalrous norms which hold that women are out of bounds as sparring partners. Moreover, if some mentally disordered offenders selectively search out weaker victims, a presumed lack of physical strength among females may make them attractive targets.

Among violent or potentially violent acts that incorporate a profit motive (that is, robbery), substance abusers stand out as heavily involved and substantial figures. These offenders (1) appear more comfortable working alone, (2) usually target lucrative commercial establishments, and (3) are likely to carry a gun, which hypothetically allows for effective control of the situation, thereby reducing the chances of physical violence.

Patterns of Violence

We now examine differences in violence across groups of offenders based on the typology we developed in chapter 2. The data indicate that felony-related violence is the most common type of violence for which offenders are imprisoned (see table 3.8). How-

---

6. Although the proportion of offenders who murder a relative is small (5 percent), we find that matricide, fratricide, and patricide occur only among offenders with psychiatric histories.

Table 3.8. Type and level of violence and eccentric offense behavior by mental health experience of offender

	Significance[a] level	Mental health experience			
		No history (n=544)	Substance abuse history (n=83)	Psychiatric history (n=540)	Substance abuse and psychiatric history (n=141)
Type of violence					
Retaliatory	.40	12.5%	10.8%	15.7%	14.4%
Unmotivated	.00	1.2	0.0	6.5	5.8
Felony-related	.00	50.8	45.8	33.7	43.9
Sex—adult victim	.00	3.7	7.2	8.5	2.9
Sex—child victim	.00	4.5	3.6	10.7	0.7
Weapon	.00	8.7	3.6	2.0	5.0
Arson	.17	1.2	2.4	3.1	2.9
Police victim	.31	1.7	3.6	2.8	0.7
Burglary	.02	13.1	21.7	14.4	22.3
Auto/ institution	.82	2.3	1.2	2.4	1.4
Level of violence					
No violence	.11	18.9%	20.5%	15.9%	24.5%
Less serious	.00	33.6	43.4	21.1	35.3
Serious	.03	30.3	22.9	31.5	20.1
Extreme	.00	17.2	13.3	31.5	20.1
Eccentric offense behavior					
Ineffectual	.00	3.5%	8.4%	10.9%	10.6%
Frenzied	.00	1.8	2.4	9.8	8.5
Symptomatic	.00	1.8	0.0	7.8	4.3
No motive	.00	1.1	1.2	8.0	4.3
No memory	.00	1.3	10.8	6.1	13.5

[a]Chi-square, specified category versus all others.

ever, proportions of felony-related violence vary across groups, ranging from half of the comparison group to one-third of the psychiatric group. The second most common offense type is burglary, which most people would consider a property crime. As before, we again find that burglars are disproportionately represented among substance abusers. Specifically, more than a fifth of the substance abusers (both groups) are burglars, which is about one and a half times the proportion of burglars in other offender groups. The next most common type of violence is retaliatory violence, and the proportion of inmates in this category does not differ significantly across groups.

The remaining violence types are relatively uncommon but show significant variations across groups. Both groups of inmates with a history of psychiatric problems more frequently engage in unmotivated violence, which includes situations in which the offender cannot offer plausible explanations for his or her act. Although only 6.5 percent of the incidents committed by the psychiatric patients can be described as unmotivated violence, the proportion is five times greater than that of the comparison group. The difference is important because unmotivated attacks are by definition enigmatic, unpredictable, and undeserved and therefore are viewed as extremely threatening. Many unmotivated attacks are dramatically newsworthy and are often portrayed as characteristic of disturbed offenders. Thus, the results of our analysis are significant on two counts. First, we find that disturbed offenders hold a near monopoly on unmotivated violence. Yet we also find that such incidents are relatively infrequent and can hardly be described as characteristic of the type of violence committed by disturbed offenders.

The two disturbed offender groups are also more likely to commit sexual violence, against both adults and children. The proportion of sex offenders is substantial in that it amounts to nearly one-fifth of the psychiatric group. Inmates with substance abuse problems are more frequently sentenced for sexual violence, but only with adult victims. The differences are significant because it is often assumed that sex offenders have peculiar motivations and, in particular, that the behavior of child molesters is pathological.

Finally, we see that the comparison group is more often convicted of weapon offenses, and that the distribution of crimes involving arson, violence against police, violence in an institution, and assault with an automobile does not vary across offender groups, although there is an indication of a difference for arson.

Possibly our most important finding is that seriousness of violence ratings shows substantial variation across mental health background. In nearly one-third of the offenses by persons with psychiatric histories the level of violence is extreme. The proportion is the highest among offender groups, being almost twice that of the comparison group. If we combine ratings of serious and extreme violence, almost two-thirds (63 percent) of incidents by offenders with psychiatric histories fall in this category, indicating that emotionally disturbed offenders are disproportionately involved with the most violent and most injurious crimes handled by the criminal justice system.

Other analyses we conducted show that recency of psychiatric problems is associated with extremity of violence. Among offenders who received psychiatric services at time of conviction, more than three-quarters (77 percent) engaged in serious or extreme violence. We infer from the data that many contemporaneously disordered offenders are seriously violent, but this conclusion should be tempered by the observation that perceived need for treatment can be influenced by degree of violence. However, while we acknowledge the possibility that persons are adjudged in need of treatment because they are violent, our analysis of career patterns showed that most offenders who became patients at conviction had mental health records predating the offense, which weakens the argument that violence is a contaminating diagnostic criterion. We also note that the proportion of serious or extreme violence for offenders with a recent psychiatric history is 66 percent and for those with a remote history, 61 percent. These findings again suggest that among offender populations recency of emotional problems increases the likelihood of serious violence.

In contrast, we see that inmates with substance abuse problems mostly engage in offenses that involve little or no violence, although this finding might be anticipated from previous analyses which showed that these offenders frequently engaged in burglary. It is also significant that violence levels among substance abusers with psychiatric problems are not greater than those among other substance abusers and are lower than those among other psychiatric patients.

On the other hand, the role of alcohol and drugs stands out in violence by offenders with substance abuse problems. Sixty percent of those with alcohol or drug problems and 64 percent of those with both psychiatric and substance problems were described as under the influence of intoxicating agents at the time of their offense. These proportions compare with 38 percent of the psychiatric group and 27 percent of the comparison group who were intoxicated under similar circumstances.

The findings on violence by substance abusers are interesting because they both confirm and dispel popular images of criminalized drug addicts. On the one hand, substance abuse is associated with increased propensities for acquisitive crimes such as burglary, and presumably these offenses are attractive because they can help underwrite the costs of addiction. We also see that many substance abusers commit crimes while under the influence of drugs or alcohol, which suggests that intoxicating agents can play a facilitative criminogenic role by lowering inhibitions. In contrast, the relatively nonserious violence levels of substance abusers do not support a view of addicts as wildly violent offenders, and the data do not support observations made by some psychiatrists that mentally ill substance abusers are especially violent.[7] As we read case files, we were struck by the number of situations in which substance abusers were impaired by alcohol or drugs to the point where they failed to behave as rational offenders or were unable to successfully carry out an offense. We include ineffective, counterproductive acts under the heading of eccen-

---

7. In a recent newspaper article, a psychiatrist, in discussing a delusional patient who was shot while attacking a police officer, stated, "He has severe mental illness, he has substance abuse, and that tends to precipitate the breakdown or make the breakdown more violent" (*New York Times*, September 23, 1988, p. B4). Of course, our data do not provide a rigorous test of this hypothesis, since not all offenders in the combined substance abuse–psychiatric group were necessarily disordered and using chemical agents about the time of the offense.

tric offense behavior, and we now return to table 3.8 to examine patterns of eccentricities among offenders in the samples.

Patterns of Eccentricity

Eccentric violence is rare among members of the comparison group, with ineffectual behavior, the most frequently appearing item, characterizing only 3.5 percent of conviction offenses. Proportions of all incidents showing other types of eccentricity fall under 2 percent. In comparison, substance abuse offenders display more ineffectual or counterproductive behavior (8.4 percent), and often claim to have no memory of the criminal event (10.8 percent). The most consistent pattern we find is that offenders with psychiatric histories are overrepresented in all categories of peculiar offense behavior. The pattern is a dramatic one, given that many violent incidents by psychiatric patients demonstrate ineffectual or counterproductive behavior, such as leaving behind incriminating evidence (10.9 percent), violent overkill or other behavior reflecting a frenzied mental state (9.8 percent), and conduct one generally thinks of as symptomatic of mental disorder (7.8 percent). In 8.0 percent of violent incidents there was no plausible motivation for the offense, while in 6.1 percent the offender could not recall his or her crime. Offenders with combined substance abuse and psychiatric problems showed the greatest difficulty recollecting details of their offenses (13.5 percent of incidents). This group is also overrepresented in other categories of eccentricity, but less so for motiveless and symptomatic violence when compared to the psychiatric group.

When we look at the relative incidence of eccentric features across mental health backgrounds, we see that the differences are substantial. Compared to offenders with no treatment history, violence by former psychiatric patients is roughly three times more likely to involve frenzied behavior, four times more likely to display symptomatic behavior, five times more likely to involve no memory of the offense, and seven times more likely to show no apparent motivation. In our opinion, the consistently disproportionate display of eccentric offense behaviors among former psychiatric patients, and in particular of symptomatic nuances, argues for recognition of "symptomatic violence," meaning situations in which clinically relevant attributes can be implicated in the violence picture of disturbed offenders. In this regard, we find that a history of emotional problems can influence violent behavior in dramatically different ways. Emotional disorders can reduce a person's competence as a violent offender, and they can also increase the damage that is done in acts of blind rage.

We thus conclude that a view of mental illness and criminality as unrelated independent attributes is not appropriate for some patient-offenders. The argument for a more integrated perspective is strongest in cases where symptoms and violence coincide, and we will take a closer look at offenses of this kind. We also conclude that two contrasting images—that of the ineffectual criminal and that of the frenzied violent offender—emerge from descriptions of offenses by disturbed individuals. Such combinations of person-related attributes and offense-related attributes deserve further scrutiny, which is a principal goal of our cluster analysis.

Types of Offenders that Emerged through Cluster Analysis

We shall next turn to the cluster analysis, which yielded types highlighting sharp contrasts on consequential variables. In reviewing these clusters, we shall see differences in types of offense, level of violence, and criminal and violence history. Substance abusers will be often differentiated by diverse histories of drug or alcohol abuse. Within offense categories (burglary, robbery, extreme personal violence) types will be seen to differ on historical variables—such as presence or absence of violence records—and demographics (for example, age). Such distinctions are gratifying in view of the number of variables we clustered, which could combine in impressively messy ways given their substantial heterogeneity.

We shall describe the content of the clusters in detail in subsequent chapters and illustrate the types of offenders who are comprised in each of these clusters.

Chapter 4

Offenders with Histories of
Mental Health Problems

We have noted that our core sample comprises former clients of mental health services, excluding substance abuse services. Cluster analysis subdivided this sample into ten diverse types (table 4.1). These types ranged widely in terms of the seriousness of the violence the offender had perpetrated and they differed in the extent to which professional interventions were deemed necessary after the offender was arrested. As we might expect, the offenders had substantial histories of mental health contacts, and in most of the groups they also had histories of violence.

Impulsive Burglars

The first type we isolated stands out because it is one whose members are not violent offenders (fifty-four of fifty-six are convicted burglars), though four of ten have committed violence in the past. The offenders are mostly young, and a surprising number (over half) were intoxicated at the time of their offense.

We call members of this group impulsive burglars because (1) they are nonprofessionals who (2) demonstrate mixed motives for burglary offenses which are often ineffective and self-destructive and (3) reflect long-term difficulties.

A case in point is that of an eighteen-year-old man imprisoned

Table 4.1. Results of cluster analysis for offenders with psychiatric histories

	Impulsive Burglar (n = 56)	Impulsive Robber (n = 39)	Long-term Explosive Robber (n = 53)	Young Explosive Robber (n = 40)	Mature Mugger (n = 22)	Acute Disturbed Exploder (n = 51)	Chronic Disturbed Exploder (n = 90)	Disturbed Sex Offender (n = 65)	Composite Career Offender (n = 60)	Compensatory Offender (n = 19)
Offense type										
Unmotivated	0%	0%	0%	0%	0%	26%	19%	5%	0%	0%
Retaliatory	0	5	2	8	0	51	39	8	5	11
Felony-related	0	74	85	75	100	12	7	9	17	58
Sex—adult victim	0	10	2	5	0	2	19	14	8	11
Sex—child victim	0	3	6	8	0	2	4	43	20	11
Weapon	2	0	0	0	0	0	0	5	12	0
Arson	2	5	2	3	0	0	0	12	3	11
Police victim	0	0	4	3	0	6	3	3	5	0
Burglary	96	0	0	0	0	0	0	0	28	0
Auto/institution	0	3	0	0	0	2	9	2	2	0
Violence level										
No violence	98%	0%	0%	0%	0%	0%	0%	5%	35%	0%
Less serious	0	62	50	53	100	0	0	0	10	11
Serious	2	21	47	43	0	0	0	89	52	90
Extreme	0	18	4	5	0	100	100	6	3	0
Alcohol/drug influence	55%	44%	34%	33%	32%	22%	46%	31%	32%	47%
Eccentricity										
Ineffectual behavior	7%	5%	8%	8%	5%	29%	11%	11%	12%	21%
Frenzied mental state	0	3	2	3	0	35	30	2	0	5
Symptomatic behavior	0	5	4	0	0	29	8	14	3	11
No apparent motive	2	3	2	0	0	29	18	9	0	0
No memory	5%	5%	3%	0%	5%	10%	10%	6%	5%	11%
Psychotic diagnosis	5	5	23	5	23	53	28	25	37	53
	9	5	20	25	23	22	22	20	18	53

Table 4.1. Continued

	Impulsive Burglar (n = 56)	Impulsive Robber (n = 39)	Long-term Explosive Robber (n = 53)	Young Explosive Robber (n = 40)	Mature Mugger (n = 22)	Acute Disturbed Exploder (n = 51)	Chronic Disturbed Exploder (n = 90)	Disturbed Sex Offender (n = 65)	Composite Career Offender (n = 60)	Compensatory Offender (n = 19)
Violence history										
None	63%	100%	0%	0%	27%	59%	0%	85%	2%	5%
Recent	27	0	47	88	27	24	47	6	27	68
Remote	18	0	100	33	55	18	94	9	98	42
Arrest history										
Low	32%	87%	4%	40%	23%	67%	7%	51%	2%	42%
Medium	48	13	4	45	64	28	28	35	37	58
High	20	0	93	15	14	6	66	14	62	0
Psychiatric history										
Instant	27%	28%	19%	10%	23%	78%	31%	65%	37%	84%
Recent	41	28	40	28	46	53	41	32	37	79
Remote	70	67	85	83	73	55	89	63	93	79
Age										
Low	68%	82%	13%	98%	0%	0%	13%	15%	0%	11%
Medium	29	13	68	3	100	53	46	37	8	84
High	4	5	19	0	0	47	41	48	92	5
Prison experience	18%	0%	59%	8%	18%	2%	51%	14%	73%	16%
Under supervision	32	15	36	45	32	10	24	12	30	37
Covariates										
Single	77%	95%	77%	90%	76%	80%	63%	77%	59%	94%
High school graduate	25	13	26	0	14	33	21	25	34	33
White	60	31	42	23	29	35	31	60	45	26
Employed	71	54	73	58	68	71	67	71	86	67

for a spree of four burglaries, in which he stole mostly jewelry. The offender's problems began early with learning disabilities compounded by anxiety and destructiveness. Antisocial acts in school included disruption of classes and theft of a teacher's purse. There was also a burglary (at age thirteen) involving an abandoned building. A year later there was another burglary in which the offender broke into a house and stole jewelry and a pair of socks; he was placed in a residential program, from which he absconded. This sequence was followed by other burglaries, other residential placements, and more escapes.

For his last offenses the man was placed in the Job Corps. Staff reported that "he had numerous behavioral problems" and added the following examples of his behavior record while at Job Corps:

> Assaulted another student with a chair during an argument over a candy cane.
>
> Carried two small cans of gasoline to the dorm with the idea of setting the dorm on fire.
>
> Numerous fights with other male students over trivial matters.
>
> Suspected of being involved in a break-in of a center residence and the center canteen.

The offender was jailed and soon required mental health services. The jail staff reported that

> he was hospitalized twice in the Forensic Unit of the County Jail because of suicidal potential. First admission was after he attempted to hang himself in the bullpen with his shoelaces. He was discharged in an improved condition [and] was re-admitted because a noose was found in his cell and he threatened to kill himself in order not to go to state prison. On second admission he also exhibited psychotic symptoms, an underlying schizophrenic condition.

The offender ascribed his suicide attempts to difficulties he experienced in obtaining drugs. The same passive, infantlike stance characterized the man when he entered prison, where staff complained that he "seems to be lacking in . . . motivation."

A similarly nonprofessional flavor permeates a second case, that of a twenty-three-year-old burglar. This man's difficulties began at age six and included "family problems." Among these were a sadistic, abusing father, who "used to beat him and handcuff him to his bed or a back porch railing," and a half-brother who sexually abused him.

One site the man burglarized was a program from which he had received services. He also broke into the home of a friend who had helped him with legal fees, clothing, and shelter. The man appeared unable to refrain from committing offenses when placed on probation and parole, requiring that he be institutionalized. A social worker observed that "he seems almost to want to be punished or at least caught, particularly in light of his constant, flagrant violations of probation and curfew." The offender himself said that he was "a person who can be talked into anything" and claimed he was "afraid someday someone will talk him into killing someone." Such statements are revealing because they were not designed to invite lenient dispositions despite their disarming honesty and self-effacement.

Impulsive Robbers

Impulsive robbers are very youthful robbers who have no histories of violent crimes and negligible criminal histories. Like impulsive burglars, such young offenders have childhood problems, including mental health problems.

The pattern is illustrated by a twenty-year-old man serving his first prison sentence for robbery after he broke into an occupied house, whose owner he threatened and manhandled but did not seriously hurt. The offender had been a drug and alcohol abuser, and he was intoxicated at the time of the offense. He had also been a long-term patient, having been hospitalized for eight years starting at age eleven. He had most recently committed himself to a hospital after seeing his mother stabbed by her boyfriend and had to be rehospitalized as soon as he arrived in prison.

The offender had been a victim of child abuse and had been brain-injured in infancy. He is virtually illiterate and is borderline mentally retarded. He is also psychotic and claims he heard voices that instructed him to hurt himself and other people.

The man is easily intimidated, which caused him many problems in prison. Other problems had to do with his impulsive aggressivity, which impelled him to assault other inmates and destroy furniture. However, the man was deathly afraid of guards (he thought they would beat him for "not making his bed right") and invited exploitation by peers, to which he then clumsily reacted.

This offender's prison career consisted of transfers between the prison hospital (where his deportment improved under medication) and disciplinary segregation settings. As a result of this pattern his chances for program involvement became slim and his prospects of community adjustment negligible.

This offender is somewhat more disturbed than most impulsive robbers but typifies this group in his combination of youthfulness, rootlessness, and inadequacy, which augurs an inauspicious career.

Long-Term Explosive Robbers

Long-term disturbed robbers are older robbers who have high arrest records and extensive histories of violence. They also have longstanding mental health problems and have led checkered—and singularly unsuccessful—careers. Many (30 percent) are intellectually deficient.

One robbery offender who typifies this serious and obdurate pattern is a twenty-eight-year-old man who had evolved a propensity for beating women during the process of stealing their pocketbooks. He explained that he had to assault his victims because they refused to part with their bags. He further indicated that he covets bags "because my mother has money in her pocketbook all the time." He also explained that he did not victimize men "because I don't want them to come after me."

The offender is a chronic schizophrenic who had been hospitalized frequently. He is mentally retarded and was described by prison staff as "simplistic, polite and cooperative." Despite his extensive offense history (ten prior felony arrests) and his predatory crimes, the man had to be placed in protective, structured settings, where he did well under continuing medication.

Another twenty-eight-year-old robber had been arrested nineteen times in ten years. He had most recently robbed a supermarket at knifepoint and resisted arrest, injuring a police officer. In a prior offense he had entered a cookie store, demanding samples, and had assaulted a customer who turned her back on him and "didn't apologize."

The offender had been committed to several different hospitals and on one occasion had been found incompetent to stand trial. He had also attempted suicide. In prison the man was described as "bizarre, babbling, and [showing an] incoherent speech pattern." When he was not in hospital, the man "dwelled on the subject of masturbation inordinate amounts of time," refused to wash, and "presented a fire problem." Such deficits are typical of the group and make such men odd exemplars of hardened recidivism.

Young Explosive Robbers

Young disturbed robbers have violence histories but have not served time in prison, though they are often on probation when they are arrested. These robbers also tend to commit offenses which involve appreciable levels of violence, if one considers the extreme youthfulness (98 percent young) of the cluster.

One offender fitting this precocious category is a volatile nineteen-year-old man who served his first prison term for a robbery with a sawed-off shotgun. Like other young robbers, this man had been raised in a succession of institutions, starting with special schools in which he had to be placed after he failed kindergarten. He did not do better in such special schools, from which he was mostly suspended for temper tantrums in which he attacked teachers and fellow students.

Some settings would not accept the man because he was explosive, and others discharged him after they discovered they could not accommodate his explosions. The man was also a problem because he is badly retarded (his IQ is 63) and has emotional instability which yields imperfectly to medication.

The man had been arrested twice for criminal assaults and had served time in a youth institution for robbing an elderly woman at knife point. After he was released from this placement, the man pistol-whipped an acquaintance and committed the shotgun robbery for which he was incarcerated. He arrived in prison announcing that he had enemies among fellow inmates, though he refused to tell staff who they were.

A second young offender stands convicted of a mugging in which the victim was knocked down before he was robbed of his possessions. The man had spent eight years in psychiatric settings, first as a young child, with the notation that "[his] hospitalization has been made necessary as a result of hyperactivity, unmanageable behavior, assaultiveness and aggressiveness toward smaller children." He was thereafter diagnosed as suffering from childhood schizophrenia and organic brain damage with impaired intellectual functioning; he did not do well on a trial release from the hospital, during which he assaulted members of his family.

The man's last conviction involved a car theft, for which he was sentenced to nine months in jail. In prison, the man was deemed victim-prone because he is retarded, but he saw himself as tough and picked fights with other inmates.

The combined aggressivity and vulnerability of young explosive robbers create a problem for prisons, which is exacerbated by the fact that the offenders (not one of whom has graduated from high school) have remedial programing needs.

The Mature Mugger

Mature muggers are a contrasting group of offenders of median age who commit robberies involving nonserious violence—typically the sorts of crimes committed by younger offenders.

One example is a thirty-five-year-old man who had mugged a woman and was cornered by her neighbors. He explained that he "had more than his two-drink limit," had discovered he was "feeling very hungry," and "knew there was no food at home." He also testified that he "saw the victim, who was nicely dressed, and thought she would have some money and that 'it wouldn't hurt her if I took a couple of dollars.'" He explained that he had once attempted a similar offense under similar circumstances, and "some men saw what happened and chased me and beat me up."

The man had been hospitalized on thirteen occasions, for periods from one week to one month, diagnosed as suffering from paranoia and depression. He indicated that whenever he felt the onset of such an episode, he would walk to the hospital and commit himself. A probation officer suggested that "the defendant seems to need the hospital at times for a complete rest and the security and the extra care it gives him. He also likes their food."

Hospital staff wrote that the man was "generally nonviolent and extremely passive-dependent . . . respectful of authority figures and trusting of them and very cooperative in our program." They also testified that the man "recompensates quickly while in the hospital and usually responds well to medication and milieu therapy."

The offender is childlike. He had made no effort to earn a living; he had no plans to work. When questioned about his future, he could envisage only "starvation ahead."

A second mugger used an unloaded gun to threaten pedestrians, explaining that he "didn't know how to load it." The man's IQ ranged between 43 and 59, depending on who had tested him. He had been treated for brain damage in childhood. He had also been treated for "a tendency toward explosive, rather bizarre behavior" which consisted of setting his mother's bed on fire and threatening to shoot other relatives.

In prison the man was placed in a special program. Here he did well, and staff reported that other "inmates on the block appeared to like [him] and made special efforts to protect him." Later, staff wrote, "He carries out simple tasks well. . . . He has developed a cooperative attitude and a willingness to please those in authority. He has made lesser progress in the area of personal hygiene and grooming skills and needs reminders to wash his clothes."

The man managed prison as a result of the tender care he was afforded. Prison staff explained that "he gets around by following the person in front of him; new situations can't be handled." Staff concluded that "it is unlikely that he would be able to manage without assistance," which means that "he will always need a sheltered, supervised program and may prove unable to function in an unsupervised living situation."

Acute Disturbed Exploders

The types we have designated disturbed exploders are invariably dangerous offenders and perpetrate extreme—and often bizarre—violence. The acute disturbed exploder group contains inmates who are often diagnosed psychotic, are viewed as disturbed at the time of arrest, and commit eccentric offenses. Two-thirds of these inmates, however, have low arrest records, and half have no histories of violence, despite the fact that the group tends to be relatively old. Its violence is thus late-blooming.

Fairly typical of exploders is a twenty-six-year-old schizophrenic convicted of manslaughter. The man had no offense history but as a youth became fearful and led a reclusive life. His relatives reported that he "even had tar put on the roof, thinking that if someone wanted to get him they would get stuck in the tar."

This history is significant because before he committed his last crime the man reexperienced the onset of his delusions:

> He started talking about drug dealers, big crime and the communists taking over. . . . A few days before the shooting his mother stated that he asked her if she had heard a van pulling into the driveway at about 3 AM, claiming that some people in the van wanted him to come outside so that they could shoot him. . . . He used to hide . . . putting pillows on his bed so that people would think that he was there.

The man's delusions focused on gangs of drug dealers, and he decided to kill a person he suspected of such membership. He could not find his intended victim, however, and shot one of the man's associates. Thereafter he attempted suicide in the jail, had to be hospitalized, and assaulted a nurse in the hospital. In prison he continued to be fearful and complained of psychosomatic problems. Staff reported that "he became suspicious, thought the Mafia was after him, and that his father was going to kill him with a gun. He became inappropriate, tense, unable to sleep and had little appetite, as he felt someone was trying to poison his food."

At other times the man's delusions took a more ethereal form, including a letter to the victim he had killed expressing his remorse and revealing that he had become concerned about space invaders:

> In discussing his delusions he indicates that FBI agents and drug dealers are no longer the source of his difficulties, but that through the assistance of another inmate he has been able to see that certain human beings are, in fact, space creatures who have been placed on

the earth and have assumed human form for the purpose of harassing and controlling certain people, of which he is one.

Throughout his tenure in prison the man functioned as a mental health client, commuting fearfully between prison clinic and hospital settings.

Another offender, also in his midtwenties, had earned no criminal record to date though he was a drug addict who had led a nomadic life, centering on residence in flophouses. In one such transient establishment the man killed a neighbor by stuffing clothing down his throat after he became convinced that this neighbor was conspiring against him. He subsequently had to be hospitalized from the jail, refused to eat, and needed to be fed through a tube. He also attempted suicide by hanging.

Released on probation, the man attacked members of his family and was resentenced to prison. He arrived in prison confused and withdrawn, refused to eat, and walked into walls, but recovered under medication. He again had to be hospitalized. Between hospitalizations the man "was not interested in any programs . . . but only liked to read magazines, newspapers and then would sit back and sleep in his chair." This is a nonviolent behavior pattern, but violence-related concerns were raised about the future because the man blamed his mother for his imprisonment and had threatened to kill her.

Chronic Disturbed Exploders

Chronic exploders are the largest cluster of disturbed offenders. They are also a distinctly violent group, both because their offenses are invariably extremely serious and because they have histories of violence. The offenders often have substantial arrest records and long-term mental health problems.

Some chronic exploders show consistency in their crimes. One offender was imprisoned for injuring four persons in a knife attack. One of the man's victims was his former spouse, whose face the offender had slashed in a previous incident. Before being sentenced for his second offense the man declared that he intended someday to kill his ex-wife (and himself) and "insisted that [his probation officer] include such statements in his report."

The offender was first institutionalized at age eleven, after he had been adjudicated a neglected child. At the time he was seen as a problem client. He maintained this reputation in the army, from which he received an undesirable discharge. He served prison time for forgery, then graduated to kidnapping. At this juncture he was adjudged disturbed and was twice declared incompetent to stand trial. After he was finally imprisoned, he spent much time in the prison hospital, where he was diagnosed "schizoid." However, he viewed himself throughout as nondisturbed. He still insisted that he had no mental health problems as he reentered prison, though he asked a psychiatrist for medication.

A second exploder was involved in a sadistic episode in which an elderly victim was stomped, beaten, sexually abused, and robbed. The man had a history of prior arrests, yielding five convictions. One of his arrests involved sexual abuse, which the man described as consensual sex with an underage girl.

The man started life in foster child placement and was hospitalized at age eight after his foster parents concluded that they could not control him. He spent five years in a hospital, where staff wrote that "he has not been able to transcend his traumatic and extremely deprived childhood. . . . At this time, the prognosis for reintegration into the community is poor."

Thereafter, the man spent twenty years leading a transient existence interspersed with crimes ranging from burglary to robbery and assault.

Disturbed Sex Offenders

This cluster contains sex offenders who mostly victimize children and are by definition responsible for serious violence. These offenders are also disturbed. They are often seen by mental health staff at the time of their offense, and one in four (28 percent) has been diagnosed as psychotic. They are older offenders, mostly Caucasian, and usually have no history of violence or of imprisonment.

One sex offender in our sample is a man in his late thirties who had victimized his daughter and infant son. He described these predations as "hug therapy" designed to prevent them from having misconceptions about sexuality. He also claimed that he had been sexually abused as a child and described himself as a practitioner of Satanism.

The man had no prior contacts with the criminal justice system. However, he had been caught smuggling marijuana in the navy and had admitted to drug and alcohol abuse. The man was upset at being arrested. He went on a protracted hunger strike in the jail, not out of guilt but because he feared prison, where he knew child molesters are unpopular. He complained that "if he had been a 'murderer or airport bomber' he would be a prison hero but due to the nature of his actions he would not do well in prison."

The man arrived at prison reception depressed and in tears and was placed in a protective setting, where he did fairly well. He was not deemed disturbed, but staff wrote that "he has a strange outlook on life." They later upgraded their views after the man attempted suicide. He had become depressed because he had been turned down by the parole board and his wife had divorced him. The parole board had suggested that the man undergo therapy, and he followed their recommendation. He was adjudged to have made progress, and no longer announced that he would kill himself after his eventual release. He also resolved his religious conflict (between Christianity and Satanism) by professing that "he tends to lean toward God."

A second sex offender resembles the first. He was imprisoned for sodomizing his daughter, attempted suicide in confinement, and had to be hospitalized from the prison. The man is in his thirties and had long-standing problems. He had been sent to a boarding school as a child because he could not be managed at home. In this institution he "alleged that during his first week he was sodomized by another boy who repeatedly sodomized him over the next five years." After leaving the institution the man was hospitalized for "nervous breakdowns." He later married, but a social worker recorded that "his attempts at leading a semblance of a normal life were unsuccessful."

The man was arrested while on probation for another sex offense involving an underage victim. He then tried to hang himself in jail, where other inmates attempted to strangle him and scald him with boiling water. He also professed guilt and alleged that his offenses "will torture me for the rest of my life."

In prison, the man had to commute between protective and mental health settings, including the prison hospital. In the hospital he was again assaulted by a fellow inmate, who also attacked him in the prison. After two serious psychotic relapses, prison staff wrote: "It appears that [this inmate] for the time being at least will continue to experience difficulties maintaining himself within the correctional system, and may well require extended psychiatric intervention."

Composite Career Offenders

The composite group contains older offenders with long-term mental health histories and long-standing records of violent involvements. The crimes these offenders commit are diverse, and most have been previously imprisoned.

The hallmark of the group (like that of long-term disturbed exploders) is that the offenders have long histories of mental health problems and records of offenses and are both career criminals and career patients. An illustrative composite career is that of an offender serving a life sentence for an armed robbery. The man is in his thirties, but he is a veteran offender who had been convicted of a burglary at age ten. His first adult offense (at sixteen) was one in which he assaulted and injured a police officer. He was subsequently convicted of rape, robberies, assaults, escapes, and weapons offenses.

After the man's arrest for robbery he was declared incompetent to stand trial and diagnosed as suffering from paranoid schizophrenia. He had also been declared incompetent and hospitalized nine years earlier. Thereafter he had been sent to prison, where staff noted that he "is severely suicidal and can act out violently when he doesn't get his way." At the time the man described his occupation as "hustling," which was accurate since he had never worked and was a multidrug user.

In prison the man had to be committed and tried to hang himself in the prison hospital. Psychiatrists there described him as psychotic. They reported that he "experiences auditory hallucinations, hears his mother's voice calling him different names, feels there are spies out to kill him, was autistic and withdrawn, appeared slovenly and dirty." Yet the man made a recovery, left prison, and reembarked on his criminal career.

The man reentered prison denying his criminal history and "claim[ing] he is the victim of racial prejudice." He also declared that he would not participate in programs since he had been unjustly incarcerated. He nonetheless did well in prison programs, was well regarded by staff, and appeared to have found a long-term home.

Compensatory Offenders

This small cluster of very disturbed persons comprises chronically disadvantaged offenders, over half of whom (ten of nineteen) have been diagnosed psychotic. These offenders tend to have clear-cut intellectual deficiencies, mostly commit serious violence (often robberies), and have histories of violence. They tend to be intoxicated and ineffectual at the time of their offense. They lead a rootless and isolate existence, as exemplified by the fact that eighteen of nineteen are unmarried, though few of them are young.

The crimes of this group reflect the multiple inadequacies of its members. A typical incident is described as follows: "The instant offense finds [the offender] under the influence of alcohol and drugs, cutting the purse strap of a seventy-one (71) year-old female, knocking her to the ground and stealing the purse." The offender was described at prison entry as "a high school graduate with no work history due to a psychiatric disability [who] has been diagnosed as a paranoid schizophrenic, which has been somewhat exacerbated by alcohol abuse."

The man was hospitalized when in his teens and maintained on medication. Prison staff diagnosed him as a schizophrenic in remission with a "passive aggressive personality" and learning problems. They suggested counseling and remedial education.

A parallel offender assaulted a seventy-year-old man, returned to the scene, and was caught. Before the offender was sentenced he was subjected to a competency examination because he is severely retarded. He is also a school dropout, had been hospitalized (diagnosed as manifesting "schizophrenia, latent type"), and had been an admitted alcohol and drug addict. He had not been in prison before but had an offense history consisting of aborted muggings.

A third offender set fires which "appear to be an attention-getting device." He did so when he was intoxicated, which he was very often. After his last fire, he gave himself up to the police. The offender is retarded and has hallucinations, for which he had been hospitalized. He had committed offenses other than arson (none major), which he also attributed to intoxication.

Reconstituting Humpty Dumpty

The vignettes illustrate differences among clusters but also highlight the continuum of which the clusters form part. This is so because violent offenders often have multiple problems and present similar dilemmas to service providers. Among the features these individuals—irrespective of type—seem to share are (1) the advent of symptoms and/or behavior problems at early ages leading to (2) early institutional placement followed by (3) ad seriatim institutionalization and (4) an unproductive, marginal, migratory existence which includes (5) brushes with the law. The offenders often (6) have combinations of deficits, such as emotional problems exacerbated by substance abuse, which (7) color some of their offenses, raising questions of competence, and (8) impair their ability to manage in prison and profit from prison programs; this (9) decreases their prospects of successful community adjustment, thus (10) increasing the chances of recidivism, including (11) violent recidivism.

Other links between the clusters are more specific. One such link has to do with the fact that age-specific clusters can be career junctures which follow each other in time. Impulsive robbers can thus become long-term robbers, and impulsive burglars can turn into composite career offenders, given time. Levels of violence and pathology can also change, separately or in tandem. Acute exploders, for example, are typically late bloomers, both as offenders and patients. Long-term robbers, by contrast, often deescalate one or both elements of their careers.

Chapter 5

Offenders with Substance Abuse Histories

Chapter 4 surveyed violent offenders with histories of mental health problems, and this chapter extends the review. We again examine offenders who have received services in the community, but we now view persons for whom services include treatment for substance abuse problems. In the second half of this chapter we turn to clients of exclusively specialized services.

The difference between offenders who receive substance abuse services and the offenders we have already discussed is admittedly one of degree, since emotionally disturbed offenders often report abusing drugs or alcohol. The substance abuse histories we review in the present chapter, however, are more salient. They also contain more detail, thus permitting disaggregation by type of substance abuse. More important, the data we have about alcohol or drug addiction over time can be used as a disaggregating criterion, so that types can be based on the offender's long-term and short-term history of substance abuse.

The Mental Health–Substance Abuse Sample

Our first (compound) sample contains recipients of both specialized and nonspecialized services. The sample, as noted in our summary typology (table 5.1), yielded five clusters.

Table 5.1. Results of cluster analysis for offenders with compounded substance abuse and psychiatric histories

	Dependent Burglar (n = 20)	Skid Row Robber (n = 9)	Skid Row Exploder (n = 35)	Compounded Career Offender (n = 37)	Multi-problem Robber (n = 28)
Offense type					
Unmotivated	0%	0%	6%	16%	0%
Retaliatory	0	0	37	14	4
Felony-related	0	100	11	54	71
Sex—adult victim	0	0	6	5	0
Sex—child victim	15	0	0	0	4
Weapon	0	0	9	3	0
Arson	0	0	9	3	0
Police victim	0	0	3	0	0
Burglary	85	0	17	3	21
Auto/institution	0	0	3	3	0
Violence level					
No violence	95%	0%	20%	3%	21%
Less serious	5	89	9	43	57
Serious	0	11	31	40	18
Extreme	0	0	40	24	4
Alcohol/drug influence	65%	89%	80%	54%	46%
Eccentric behavior	10	11	29	32	14
Psychotic diagnosis	5	11	6	27	7
No memory	10	22	23	8	14
Low IQ	20	0	17	8	14
Violence history					
None	25%	0%	9%	5%	75%
Recent	20	11	43	30	14
Remote	70	100	71	89	14
Arrest history					
Low	5%	0%	17%	0%	61%
Medium	15	11	43	27	39
High	80	89	40	73	0
Psychiatric history					
Instant	25%	11%	26%	14%	25%
Recent	25	33	60	27	32
Remote	85	78	54	92	68

Table 5.1. *Continued*

	Dependent Burglar (n = 20)	Skid Row Robber (n = 9)	Skid Row Exploder (n = 35)	Compounded Career Offender (n = 37)	Multi-problem Robber (n = 28)
Drug history					
None	10%	89%	86%	0%	43%
Recent	55	11	14	19	25
Remote	50	0	0	87	36
Alcohol history					
None	85%	0%	6%	89%	64%
Recent	10	33	57	5	21
Remote	5	89	54	5	18
Age					
Low	0%	0%	14%	3%	39%
Medium	65	0	49	46	36
High	35	100	37	51	25
Prison experience	50%	89%	37%	73%	4%
Under supervision	50	22	31	32	25
Covariates					
Single	60%	44%	86%	62%	86%
High school graduate	10	22	21	27	25
White	75	67	54	49	61
Employed	90	89	88	81	85

Dependent Burglars

Like all our inmate samples, the compound sample includes a group of burglars whose offenses are invariably nonviolent. But burglars with mental health and substance abuse problems are a distinctive group. For one, they tend to be older and Caucasian, and they have substantial arrest records. Most of the offenders also have long-term histories of violent involvements and of mental health contacts, they have been treated for drug addiction, and more than half (thirteen of twenty) are intoxicated when they commit their burglaries.

An offender who provides an illustrative case is a twenty-eight-year-old man who burglarized a neighbor. He committed this visible offense, according to a person who interviewed him, because "at the time he was high after taking three quaaludes and smoking PCP, [and] because of his intoxicated state he got an urge to get up and steal." The man claimed complete lack of premeditation. In further exoneration, he pointed out that his performance was clearly substandard, arguing that "if this was planned, I would have used gloves."

The man had never used gloves. His difficulties had begun in early childhood (when his recorded IQ was 67, though he later tested at 102), and he took up drugs at age twelve. He ambivalently boasted that he averaged ten marijuana cigarettes daily, that he had used angel dust for a decade and "had taken over one hundred LSD trips." These facts matter to us because the man engages in circular reasoning, in which he attributes his problems to his addiction and his addiction to his problems. He reported that he failed parole because "I can't do it on my own . . . the pressures are unbelievable." He absconded from drug treatment, he said, because "weekly contacts are not enough," and he engaged in group offenses because of an "inability to separate himself from a negative peer group."

The offender had been a penny ante recidivist. He served an earlier prison sentence for an aborted burglary in which he was intoxicated. He later had problems in prison which included being caught in the act of injecting himself with drugs. Prison staff complained about the man's "supercilious attitude and perceived macho/gangster type image" but protected him from his peers, who filled him with anxiety. The dilemma faced by the staff was that the man proved to be a shamelessly dependent person who relied on outside support (which is unhealthy), but that one had to reinforce his pattern, like it or not, because he could not manage without support. The same dilemma was faced by the man's parents, who "on numerous occasions bailed him out of jail, paid his legal fees and allowed him to remain in their house," nevertheless earning his ingratitude.

A similar dependency problem pattern is that of a second burglar who took little responsibility for his acts. The man was a substantial recidivist who had committed a rape, which he loudly disclaimed. He also minimized his last offense—he was caught burglarizing—by maintaining that "he was really only a bystander." After this burglary offense the man attempted suicide in jail and was hospitalized (in installments) for close to a year.

The man's criminal career was continuous starting in grade school, where he had stolen from purses, mailboxes, and desks, and had urinated in classrooms. He had also deployed more blatant attention-getting measures, such as having intercourse with an inflatable dummy used as a demonstration device in health classes.

The man is an addict who had ingested a variety of drugs (he had even inhaled gasoline fumes). He did not care to have anyone deal with this problem, however. According to the record, he "absconded from a drug program because the stress of facing issues relating to his drug use and emotional problems was too much." Mental health staff also classed the man as treatment-resistant and reported that he "had a problem keeping appointments."

The offender's entry into prison proved inauspicious because he took the view that he "couldn't do a maximum security sentence, as he would be killed." He lived for much of his time in prison protection cells and invested most of his effort arranging transfers between prisons. He set fire to his cell in one setting and assaulted a guard in another, while depending on guards to extricate him from environments he feared.

Skid Row Robbers

The second cluster contains few (only nine) offenders, all middle-aged alcoholics who commit robberies. The men have long offense histories, including violent offense histories, and tend to be drunk at the time they commit their offenses.

A typical group member "states that he has been drinking for twenty years and drinks a couple of six packs of beer per day and a fifth of Scotch." On the day of his last offense (an armed robbery of a cabdriver) the man had consumed five bottles of wine, and the arresting officer described him as "very, very flushed." The probation officer noted that "it is possible that the defendant really was so drunk that he didn't know what he was doing, since the arresting officer concurs with the idea that the defendant was highly intoxicated. In that case, a lifestyle of intoxication on the part of the defendant may be a primary source of his continuing criminality."

The man's extensive offense history included an arrest for assault (dismissed), two convictions for driving under the influence of alcohol, several burglaries, and an insurance violation. The man's alcohol problems had been attended to at a VA hospital (he is a Vietnam veteran), where he was detoxified "once every other year." The offender also was past president of a local chapter of Alcoholics Anonymous.

A second offender robbed a gas station, then embarked on a high-speed chase in which he threw several objects—including the proceeds of the robbery—from his car window. He was drunk at the time and reported steady drinking for some seven years, averaging a quart of alcohol a day. The offender was also a discharged veteran. Before becoming an alcoholic he had been a drug addict and minor dealer, and many of his (eighteen) arrests were drug-related, though he had also been convicted of larceny, burglary, possession of weapons, and driving while intoxicated.

The man had been diagnosed as a very serious alcoholic who suffered from "bouts of blackouts, liver and pancreatic damage." He had been treated for these conditions in a variety of programs, but the ministrations proved less than successful because the man insisted that he had no alcohol problem he could not handle. The man was a success in prison, however, where he functioned well as a skilled carpenter.

Skid Row Exploders

A contrasting pattern to that of skid row robbers is that of alcoholics whose violence is diversified and explosive. The arrest record of these offenders is often low, but the offenders tend to be seriously emotionally disturbed and tend to be drunk when they commit their crimes.

An example of such an offender is a middle-aged woman

whose difficulty (as assessed by others) consisted of the fact that "when intoxicated [she] becomes extremely hostile, abusive and profane." In a past incident this lady had become embroiled in an argument after an all-night drinking session. She was dissatisfied with the resolution of the dispute and burned down her apartment building, killing a guest (a drinking companion) whose presence she had forgotten.

The last offense she committed was similar in that she was intoxicated (she claimed she had "blacked out") and held a grudge against her victim. The victim—a female neighbor—reported that

> she [the victim] came home from work and noticed [the offender] was talking very strangely, as though in a trance. [The victim] stated [the offender] left, and she was in bed just going to sleep when there was a knock of the door. [The offender] entered with a knife in her hand and began yelling at her and calling her names. . . . [The offender] then proceeded to stab [the victim] six times.

The offender in turn blamed alcohol and testified that she "only remembers standing in the hall with a knife in her hand and [the victim] bleeding."

There had been incidents in the woman's life involving diverse brushes with the law. She had been arrested for arson, assaults, and impulsive property offenses. She had also attempted suicide and had been hospitalized for alcohol abuse and for chronic schizophrenia, for which she was medicated. She participated in treatment willingly, though she assaulted a nurse in the prison because "she did not want [her dose of thorazine] diluted with water." She also had other disciplinary problems in confinement, which had to do with "temper tantrums and arguments."

Since the offender is not intoxicated when she is in the prison, her outbursts suggest that her readiness to take offense and to respond with retaliatory rage transcends her drinking episodes. Alcohol adds obliviousness to her indifference to the consequences of her acts; intoxication also adds to her rage, and emotional problems play an aggravating role because they distort (and steeply escalate) grievances grounded in minuscule disputes.

Compounded Career Offenders

Compounded career offenders are the most disturbed of the offenders who have substance abuse and mental health problems. These offenders have long-term histories of contacts with service providers; they also have serious criminal histories, including histories of violence. In addition, the offenders suffer from long-term drug addiction.

The pattern is highlighted by a violent robber who had hurt his victim, choking her and pushing her into a wall. The man went on a mystifying rampage in which he destroyed the victim's apartment, wildly scattering her possessions as the police arrived. He staged this scene after being released from prison, where he had served time for a similar offense. During this period he was also involved in a rape.

The man is in his midthirties, but his crime and mental health problems date to an early age. He had first seen a psychiatrist at fifteen; three years later he had been hospitalized, diagnosed as a chronic schizophrenic, and certified as a drug addict. On his release he became involved in weapons offenses and was convicted of robbery.

Service providers described the man's double (or triple) problem. Juvenile workers recorded that he "impresses as a disturbed youth who relates in a hostile and withdrawn fashion." Hospital staff reported that he had to be "treated with psychotropics and was a management problem." Detention officials noted that "he had to be transported in a straitjacket from the jail to the hospital." Staff of a community drug program complained that the offender "states his interests are 'partying, basketball, getting high and fooling around.'"

The man arrived in prison "extremely surly" and "exhibited a hostile and negative attitude." Two years later, a "progress report" noted that "his horrendous custodial adjustment continues this six-month period with four reports that resulted in 225 days sentenced to keeplock. [He is] a confrontative individual who has little regard for rules and regulations and who has poor rapport with staff and is only marginally acceptable with peers."

This assessment parallels that of an earlier prison stay in which officials had complained that "the inmate's behavior constitutes a real and constant physical threat to both peers and staff in spite of 'tailor-made' programs." Though the man's eccentricity was fully recognized, the impression he made was that of a dangerous, embittered, angry, and irritable person with a gigantic chip on his shoulder rather than that of a person with mental health problems.

Multiproblem Robbers

The last group of offenders is contrasting in that they commit little serious violence, have strikingly low arrest records, and are apt to be seen as disturbed. The offenders, moreover, are likely to have salient problems involving alcohol and/or drugs.

A case in point is that of a man who was imprisoned for several robberies he had attempted while on probation. In these crimes the man used a threatening extortion note which sometimes produced money but was often disregarded. The man had this note in his possession when he encountered the police.

The offender had been arrested in the past for minor offenses but had violated probation by discontinuing drug treatment. He had undergone drug treatment repeatedly, but without success. He had also been hospitalized for depression, and had been diagnosed a paranoid schizophrenic. Such difficulties continued to manifest themselves when the man was in prison, where he had to be hospitalized. He was otherwise a despondent inmate and was described as "having some difficulty coping" with various stresses of confinement.

A second offender tried to rob a bank after drinking a good deal and taking drugs. He was not only unsuccessful but himself pointed out that "he has no recall of the offense." He regretfully noted that his "substance abuse usage had snowballed [since] he was abusing alcohol, pills and cocaine."

The offender had held respectable civilian jobs but had destroyed his career by attempting white-collar offenses. He had been depressed—possibly by self-induced failure—and had attempted suicide. He had been involved in therapy, both in and out of hospitals, since adolescence. His drinking had begun at twelve and his drug addiction at fifteen. At the time of his arrest, the man combined use of vodka, barbiturates, and cocaine, all of which he used daily.

The offender is a man with limited coping competence who approached prison as a structured treatment environment, hoping for drug rehabilitation as well as a belated college education.

Postscript

The offenders in this second sample differ from those in our other samples and also from the prison population in that the majority of these offenders are white.

The second substance abuse sample (which we turn to next) also differs from the typical state prisoner, but to a lesser degree. The sample is heterogeneous, older than average (though less so than the disturbed inmates), overrepresents white inmates (to a somewhat lesser degree), and shows the influence of alcohol or drugs in the commission of crimes.

Clients of Substance Abuse Services

Inmates in the specialized sample have received mental health services only for drug and/or alcohol problems. This offender sample contains two small clusters and two larger ones (table 5.2). The small clusters comprise inmates who are engaged in non-serious violence and have no violence histories. The larger clusters contain more violence-involved inmates, who mostly tend to be intoxicated while committing their crimes.

Addicted Burglars

The first cluster consists of burglars, some of whom are on probation at the time of their offenses. These offenders are drug addicts, and three of the eleven members of the group have problems of retardation. The offenders have arrest records, but mostly no violence histories.

The careers of these offenders are unremarkable, except for testimonials they offer to the obduracy of addiction and to the unregeneracy of otherwise unimpressive criminal careers. A case

Table 5.2. Results of cluster analysis for offenders with substance abuse histories

	Addicted Burglar (n = 11)	Addicted Robber (n = 11)	Alcohol Exploder (n = 33)	Drug Exploder (n = 20)
Offense type				
Unmotivated	0%	0%	0%	0%
Retaliatory	0	0	15	20
Felony-related	0	91	36	55
Sex—adult victim	0	0	12	5
Sex—child victim	0	0	6	5
Weapon	0	0	6	0
Arson	0	0	6	0
Police victim	0	0	6	5
Burglary	100	9	9	10
Auto/institution	0	0	3	0
Violence level				
No violence	100%	0%	12%	5%
Less serious	0	91	27	55
Serious	0	0	39	25
Extreme	0	9	21	15
Alcohol/drug influence	27%	55%	70%	27%
Eccentric behavior	0	9	27	0
No memory	0	0	24	5
Low IQ	27	9	9	10
Violence history				
None	73%	64%	21%	0%
Recent	9	18	30	40
Remote	27	18	70	85
Arrest history				
Low	9%	46%	18%	0%
Medium	55	55	39	5
High	36	0	42	95
Drug history				
None	27%	0%	70%	5%
Recent	27	27	18	15
Remote	55	82	12	90
Alcohol history				
None	73%	91%	6%	85%

Table 5.2. *Continued*

	Addicted Burglar (n = 11)	Addicted Robber (n = 11)	Alcohol Exploder (n = 33)	Drug Exploder (n = 20)
Recent	27	9	46	10
Remote	0	0	67	10
Age				
Low	9%	27%	12%	5%
Medium	82	46	36	40
High	9	27	52	55
Prison experience	18%	9%	39%	70%
Under supervision	45	27	33	40
Covariates				
Single	64%	55%	85%	40%
High school graduate	18	36	24	5
White	36	45	63	30
Employed	73	70	82	90

in point is that of a thirty-year-old man who had broken into homes. The man was intoxicated at the time of his crimes and had testified against his crime partner, whom he then regarded (correctly) as a prospective enemy.

The man is a heroin addict but had also indulged in cocaine, valium, quaaludes, and marijuana. He had been a confirmed addict since age sixteen. His sixteenth birthday also marked the beginning of his crime record, which included six arrests for criminal possession of drugs, six burglary arrests, and a conviction for driving while intoxicated. During most of the man's life he had been treated (unsuccessfully) in outpatient drug programs, as well as in a veterans' hospital. The man cooperated eagerly in such treatment and expected more of the same. He told prison authorities, for example, that he wanted to undergo drug therapy and that he intended to become a drug counselor after he was paroled.

A second addicted offender is somewhat older and was convicted of offenses he had committed while on probation. In one incident the man entered a store that someone else had broken into and stole a television set. In a second offense he sold drugs to an undercover officer, and in a third incident he burglarized a neighbor who was an acquaintance.

This ill-starred offender had started life in a reformatory, to which he was committed at age eleven (at his mother's request). Here he had spent his adolescence. He then managed to become a career addict who had a substantial habit ($100 a day) but absconded from rehabilitation programs because he saw no point in abstaining from drugs.

Addicted Robbers

The second cluster consists of addicts who commit nonserious violence and who have no records of violence and very modest criminal histories. One offender in this cluster reported that he had "a $400 to $500 a day cocaine/heroin habit." To sustain this redoubtable habit, the man participated in an attempted robbery of an Oriental health club. He had also sold counterfeit money, which had earned him a federal prison sentence. The man's arrest record was otherwise modest (a fine for driving while intoxicated and an incident involving unlawful possession of marijuana), and he had owned a business, which he had lost.

The offender had participated in several drug treatment programs, and one such program medicated him for "atypical depression" after he lost his mother. The man adduced his mother's death as a contributing factor to his crime and also pointed out that "he needed money for Christmas" and had no way to earn it.

The man's capacity for deception (and for self-deception) in the short run stood him in good stead. For a time, he became a model inmate. His deportment earned him membership in a temporary release program in which he worked as a jackhammer operator for construction company, but the privilege was promptly rescinded after he took unauthorized vacations and submitted false pay receipts.

A second, younger offender committed a street robbery while "high on marijuana and beer." The offender failed after doing well in prison. He was released on parole but repaid the confidence by mugging an eighty-three-year-old pedestrian. Drug programs found the man similarly uncooperative, but on other occasions he requested treatment as a way out of difficulties.

The man had been a precocious delinquent. After placement in a juvenile facility, he graduated to a career as an addict and burglar. (Along the way he tried other ways of sustaining his drug habit, such as stealing from his family.) The man's last probation officer commented wryly on his prospects. He concluded that the man's "degree of maladjustment, particularly along the lines of changed social attitudes, is such as to warrant a reasonable belief and expectation that [he] cannot get along without further conflict with the law."

Alcohol Exploders

Addicted offenders are unreliable persons, whereas exploders are volatile. The alcohol cluster contains violent offenders who tend to be drunk at the time they commit their offenses and often do not remember what they have done. Many of the offenders are middle-aged, two-thirds are Caucasian, and all have histories of alcoholism.

Prison intake staff wrote about one such offender that "intellectual limitations combined with his alcohol abuse and social instability appear to account for his criminal involvement." The man's career showed a penchant for driving while intoxicated and also included arrests in which the man was charged with carrying a gun. This propensity culminated in a bloody incident in which the man, while drunk, tried to kill a drinking companion with whom he had had an argument by shooting him in the head.

Another alcohol offender attacked a whole family over a traffic dispute, lacerating the father with a car antenna. The man was very drunk at the time and had a history redundant with offenses involving intoxication. One such incident was described as follows:

> A statement by [the victim] indicates that she was entertaining some friends at her home when [the offender and two companions] came to her house and insisted they were going to have a party there and drink beer that they had brought. She told them no. They got

mad and started slamming and kicking at her front door, causing it to break. They then started throwing her kids' toy wagon around the front yard yelling very loudly and throwing items at vehicles in her driveway. [The offender] then broke a window out by hitting it with his fist.

There is further evidence of explosiveness in that the offender had assaulted his daughter and had been subjected to child abuse charges based on the physical damage he had done her.

The man is an undisputed alcoholic. A disgruntled probation officer complained that "[the offender's] life style has been a continuous saga of alcohol abuse and alcohol-related criminal activity. His alcoholism has interfered with every area of his life." The officer pointed out that the offender had "consistently refused to continue alcohol treatment." The man was once placed in a halfway house for alcoholics but was soon expelled "for using marijuana." He was later terminated from a hospital program for noncooperation and left a third program because he "does not feel that he has a drinking problem."

Drug Exploders

A fourth cluster consists of drug addicts with histories of violence and criminal involvements. The offenders are inveterate recidivists, and they tend to be high on drugs at the time they commit their crimes.

A case in point involves an offender who is in his thirties and "recently specialized in armed robberies of cabdrivers." The man attacked his victims at knife point while under the influence of drugs. He was also reliably intoxicated during offenses in which he resisted arrest, and on one occasion "gunned a car toward a police officer, hitting him, causing injury to his back."

The man is a career criminal, with a dossier of arrests dating to his adolescence. He sees this criminal career as subservient to his drug career, which a prison psychiatrist described as follows:

At the age of fourteen (14) he was initiated to the drug culture—he started with smoking marijuana and later experimented with other narcotic drugs, using LSD, cocaine and amphetamines and finally became an addict to heroin. He was spending $50 a day and the funds were provided by illicit activities like stealing, burglary and robbery. He said that under the influence of heroin he felt carefree and nothing bothered him.

The man had participated in several drug programs and claimed that some had occasioned respites in his habit. He also adjusted well in prison, where he held responsible jobs and participated in therapy. Despite such involvements the man invariably recidivated, graduating from less serious to more serious offenses.

Another drug offender had committed robberies in which he held a knife to his victims' throats. He victimized acquaintances, and one of them noted that "he looked like he was on drugs, with his eyes glassy and red." Police who arrested the man confirmed this condition and discovered a hypodermic needle in his pocket.

The offender had been apprehended on eighteen occasions since his seventeenth birthday. Most of his arrests were for felonies, including some he had perpetrated shortly after leaving prison. The man had participated in methadone maintenance programs in the community. He had also been involved in drug therapy while in prison, without impact on his postgraduate career.

Vignettes such as these are typical of careers in which offenders who are seriously addicted to alcohol and/or drugs reach middle age with violence-cum-addiction patterns that are intertwined, chronic, and discouragingly recalcitrant.

Chapter 6

Offenders with No Mental Health–Related Histories

In this chapter we disaggregate our comparison sample, which contains offenders who have no record of having received mental health services—at least not in the data sources available to us. Cluster analysis subdivides the sample into eight types (table 6.1). Five of these types contain larger numbers of inmates; of these five types, four are composed of robbers. The sample contains two groups of relatively nonviolent offenders (mostly burglars) and three groups of offenders whose violence is serious.

Inexperienced Burglars

The least violence-related group in our sample is that of burglars who have low arrest histories (60 percent) and no past violent involvements (68 percent). The inexperience of these burglars surprises us because we expect nonviolent offenders to be imprisoned only as a last resort, on the strength of past felonious conduct. We infer that there must be special reasons why these offenders may appear recidivistic, such as short-term trends in their offenses or cumulative impressions that include a concern with chronic delinquency.

An example is that of a young offender who had earned one adult arrest (which was dismissed) but whose conviction covered

Table 6.1. Results of cluster analysis for offenders with no mental health history

	Inexperienced Burglar (n = 60)	Experienced Burglar (n = 38)	Acute Exploder (n = 67)	Patterned Exploder (n = 30)	Pre-career Robber (n = 73)	Early Career Robber (n = 76)	Late Career Robber (n = 50)	Generalist (n = 63)
Offense type								
Unmotivated	0%	0%	5%	0%	0%	0%	0%	0%
Retaliatory	0	0	36	87	0	3	0	13
Felony-related	0	0	15	0	99	83	96	51
Sex—adult victim	0	0	8	7	0	3	0	13
Sex—child victim	0	0	22	3	0	0	0	10
Weapon	37	37	0	0	1	7	2	0
Arson	0	0	6	0	0	0	0	3
Police victim	0	0	3	0	0	0	0	5
Burglary	63	63	0	0	0	1	2	0
Auto/institution	0	0	49	13	0	5	0	37
Violence level								
No violence	90%	95%	0%	0%	0%	4%	0%	0%
Less serious	10	5	0	0	66	66	96	0
Serious	0	0	57	7	22	22	2	89
Extreme	0	0	43	93	12	8	2	11
Alcohol/drug influence	15%	26%	39%	57%	26%	16%	16%	32%
Eccentric behavior	0	3	21	27	6	4	0	5
No memory	2	0	2	7	0	3	0	0
Low IQ	17	16	30	10	15	21	10	25

Table 6.1. *Continued*

	Inexperienced Burglar (n = 60)	Experienced Burglar (n = 38)	Acute Exploder (n = 67)	Patterned Exploder (n = 30)	Pre-career Robber (n = 73)	Early Career Robber (n = 76)	Late Career Robber (n = 50)	Generalist (n = 63)
Violence history								
None	68%	0%	99%	13%	99%	0%	0%	5%
Recent	20	13	2	43	0	75	40	35
Remote	13	97	0	67	1	45	98	84
Arrest history								
Low	60%	0%	75%	30%	90%	53%	0%	13%
Medium	33	24	22	60	8	36	46	32
High	7	76	3	10	1	12	54	56
Age								
Low	45%	3%	18%	13%	52%	86%	0%	2%
Medium	37	45	58	17	41	9	72	65
High	17	53	24	67	7	5	28	33
Prison experience	8%	79%	6%	13%	0%	20%	64%	48%
Under supervision	27	50	9	13	8	42	44	24
Covariates								
Single	66%	53%	57%	55%	81%	80%	49%	52%
High school graduate	20	16	18	24	19	12	6	10
White	34	8	22	21	16	5	10	19
Employed	81	79	81	93	79	62	88	77

three incidents in which he had broken into homes. More important, the man had a juvenile history proving to the court that low-order deterrence had never impressed him. On several occasions this youth had been arrested for burglaries while on probation, and a disgruntled probation officer observed, "The defendant, a school dropout, with a history of excessive truancy, and an unstable work record, has run away from home on at least ten separate occasions, and has a pattern of hanging out with negative companions. . . . [He] appears to have a pattern of anti-social criminal behavior."

The other side of the coin is the offender's lack of aggressivity. This is illustrated by the fact that this man had signed himself into protective custody when he arrived in prison, which confirmed the impression that he was not a hardened criminal.

A second burglar is older (twenty-two) but appeared equally non-sturdy. The man had a low IQ (77) and had been perfunctorily diagnosed as having "severe emotional problems." He had spent much of his life in reformatories and had grown up to "a rather transient existence, sleeping in cars, home-made tents, with friends and in emergency housing."

Unsavory companions involved the man in burglaries in an ancillary capacity. On his own, he had stolen cars, filed false fire alarms, and committed nuisance offenses. The man had also given the impression of being nondeterrable. Placed on probation, he was rearrested a week later; sent to jail (with probation revoked), he reoffended when paroled.

Imprisonment of such offenders responds to the perceived need for a backup option when all else has failed. It may also embody the hope that incipient careers can be short-circuited through shock effects when lesser discomforts have made an insufficient impression.

Experienced Burglars

Our second group contains burglars who are older, more recidivistic, and violence-experienced. A typical member of the group is a thirty-five-year-old man who had been caught breaking into a store. The man's prison sentence was disproportionate to his crime because he was on parole at the time of his burglary and because one of his prior offenses was a rape. His record lists nineteen other arrests and twelve convictions. Though the latter were mostly for burglary, the police viewed the man as a menace to the community.

The man had been in the army, where he had spent time combating fellow soldiers. He received an undesirable discharge but proudly recalled that he had "fought an officer and threw him through a window." After this unpromising army career the man settled into a routine of committing crimes to support a drug habit. He continued to commit crimes thereafter, despite the fact that he had discontinued drug use.

In prison the man was placed in lower-security settings, attended college classes, and underwent vocational training. The man is in his thirties and may have matured, but so far he had persevered in his chosen career as a burglar, despite the occasional lapses into more serious violence that characterizes his cluster.

The group also contains persons convicted of weapons charges. One such offender was arrested when police stopped him for speeding and discovered he had a loaded gun; he was found to be a parole violator. After the man arrived in prison, staff recorded that he "claimed no one ever got hurt in his crimes," though he had been convicted of an attempted rape. The man also recalled an episode of "delivering female masseuses to a pornography place," for which he had been arrested. The offender had spent a good portion of his forty years in prison. His crimes included armed robbery (his next-to-last offense), burglary, interstate transportation of stolen property, petit theft, assault with intent to commit rape, criminal conspiracy (prostitution), drugs, profanity, driving while intoxicated, and reckless driving.

A third member of the cluster was convicted of two burglaries. After the first burglary he was arrested with the proceeds, and the second almost cost him his life because the victim (a police officer who was a markswoman) shot him in the head. The man is in his thirties and had been a burglar since his teens. In his only violent offense (at twenty) he was convicted of arson after setting an occupied building on fire because he held a grudge. The man was intoxicated at the time of this offense. He was also described as bizarre (reporting hallucinations) and was examined to see whether he could stand trial. He was narrowly certified competent but diagnosed as suffering from an "untreated psychosis." Prison psychiatrists later found no active psychosis but classed the man as an "inadequate personality" with "past history of heroin." No one suggested that the man be treated, however, and he thus qualified to join our nondisturbed (comparison) group as a veteran offender.

Acute Exploders

The third cluster is important to us because it comprises offenders who, though they have limited arrest records and no histories of past violence, commit very serious violence. These offenders are often intoxicated when they are violent or show other signs of eccentricity. Some members of the group (30 percent) are intellectually limited, and predominant violence categories are retaliatory violence and sex offenses against children.

A somewhat typical example is a first-time felon who had been convicted of arson. The man had burned down three buildings in a row. One of the buildings was occupied at the time, and the police discovered that the man had a grudge against a young woman tenant: "The officers learned that the girlfriend of [the offender] lived in one of the buildings and that the fire marshall was informed that [the offender] had threatened to kill her and she had an Order of Protection against him." This explosive individual is a twenty-one-year-old man of borderline intelligence (his IQ is 76); he had no criminal record other than two minor drug-related arrests to warn of impending violence.

A second member of the cluster is an illegal alien whose credentials were otherwise unblemished. The man's offense covered a series of explosions which started with a minor altercation. He had argued with a passenger in a van and pursued the van and tried to stop it, displaying a counterfeit police shield. The real police appeared, however, at which point the man became helplessly enraged, and the following sequence ensued:

> [The offender] sped away, but shortly thereafter was observed deliberately driving into the side of an occupied stationary police

vehicle, causing injury to two officers. The arresting officer observed [the offender] reach for a .22 caliber handgun. [The offender] was pulled out of the car through the window and arrested after a struggle. . . . [The offender] also attempted to run down the arresting officer following a court hearing.

Paradoxically, the man required protection in prison after other inmates threatened him, which suggests that his capacity for rage is evoked by specific (and very predictable) stimuli, while other threats and affronts inspire fear and/or flight.

Patterned Exploders

The fourth cluster is relatively small, but the offenders who compose it are responsible for the most extreme acts of violence, chiefly crimes of revenge. More than half commit their violence while intoxicated; almost all have violence histories, though few (13 percent) have been imprisoned. The offenders are mostly middle-aged and respectably employed.

These offenders show consistencies, but not in the sense that they replay violent offenses. Rather, their records often describe lesser violence which in retrospect foreshadows more serious violence. By reviewing past incidents we can often infer violence-related predispositions, but such inferences must be cautiously held, given that postdiction is cheap when we already know the outcome of the story. What is safe to note is that patterned explosive offenders have violence histories which make their offenses less atypical than those of other explosive offenders.

A representative offender from this group is a fifty-year-old man who had knifed another man during a drunken argument. The man described his violence as "self-defense," though the police reported that "he stabbed [the victim] repeatedly in the back, under his arm, and in the stomach near the heart, thereby attempting to cause said complainant's death." Other indications of the man's violence-proneness are that his past arrests include assaults and a warrant for "violence and battery of a law enforcement officer."

The man is an immigrant who had moved around the country for two decades. He had not learned to speak English and was "functionally illiterate" in his native language. Combined with these educational deficits is the fact that the man's intelligence is substandard (his IQ is 76).

The man may be invoking violence to resolve debates in which his language skills prove deficient, but his more general pattern was described by prison classification analysts, who concluded that "his criminal pattern is one of assault and serious violence against persons, reportedly when under the influence of alcohol."

A second exploder has a more specialized pattern. He described his offense as "a crime of passion," though he had gone out of his way to ambush his mistress and a male friend and had shot them to death. He also tried to kill a police officer, who returned the fire and injured the man. The offender's past difficulties with the law had been few but included an arrest for assault and a sentence for attempted murder, which was revealingly attributed to "personal domestic problems."

A third patterned exploder is younger, and on probation for assault. His incident was preceded by convivial drinking and a ball game, during which an argument broke out. In the course of the argument someone punched the offender, who responded by knifing the person who had punched him. His victim narrowly missed bleeding to death.

Police pointed out that the offender and his peer group "have a long-established pattern of settling arguments with violence." This pattern appeared to have started early, in that the offender (whose intelligence is "dull normal") had been suspended from school because of constant involvement in fights.

The probation officer's summary of the man's career was that "the defendant has a predisposition toward violence, which in this case nearly resulted in a tragedy." The statement is similar to characterizations one can advance about other members of this same cluster.

Precareer Robbers

The sample contains three groups of offenders who have been convicted largely of robberies. The first group differs from the other two groups in that its members have no histories of violence or of imprisonment and nonserious records of arrests.

Despite their unblemished dossiers, precareer robbers are

often seen by the system as problem persons whose prospects are grim, as illustrated by the following assessment: "A first felony offender, the defendant's actions herein would appear to demonstrate his capacity for aggressive and reckless behavior. Accordingly the prognosis for his future societal adjustment at this time necessarily is extremely guarded."

The man about whom this was written had participated in a mugging in which the victim, who refused to part with his money, was kicked onto the tracks of a subway. This offense was obviously serious, but the man's prior offenses (trespass, criminal mischief, delinquency) were unimpressive, and his mother argued that her son was disturbed rather than delinquent. The man's peers had taken him more seriously. They had seen him as a threat and had assaulted him with a knife, injuring him. The man had reacted by trying to hang himself, and personnel in jail had to move him to protect him.

Similar profiles describe other offenders. One man (age nineteen) was involved in ad seriatim muggings, in one of which the victim was injured. The man was seen as disadvantaged by some ("the product of a broken home who displays immaturity, poor self-control, lacking in skills") but as unregenerate by others ("has not responded to discipline, therapy or probation supervision in the past . . . future prognosis in sentencing this individual is poor"). He was also described as violence-embued, such as in prison, where the record tells us that the man expressed "anger and aggression toward either staff or peers."

Novice robbers are individuals who have arrived at a critical juncture of their careers: they have not been violent offenders but impress some observers as having become violent offenders who are slated for a career of serious crime.

Early Career Robbers

Members of the second robbery cluster are uniformly young but have entered upon a robbery career and been arrested for violent offenses. One out of five has been imprisoned in the past, and many (42 percent) are on probation or parole at the time of their arrest.

The offense histories of these robbers start early, and the descriptions of their offenses are redundant. One adult criminal record, for instance, starts with the account of a team mugging in which the offender's partner "grab[bed] the victim by the neck" while the offender (age fifteen), "displaying a broken beer bottle, pointed it at the victim's face and indicated that they wanted the victim's money." Months earlier, the record describes the same offender as "acting in concert with three others, allegedly removing $35 in a gold chain and gold watch from an individual."

The man entered prison for the second time for an offense in which "acting alone, he forcibly snatched two gold chains from a female victim. . . . The victim's neck and chest were scraped as a result of this offense." Prison staff asked the man about this offense, and he explained that he used angel dust every day and that this habit is expensive.

Like other members of the early career cluster, the man had spent much time in institutions and had been a recalcitrant client. The first juvenile setting to which he had been sent (after stealing from his mother) complained that "the resident exhibited a negative pattern . . . many conflicts with both staff and residents, abusive language, destructive behavior, and frequent indulgences in marijuana." A second setting reported that "he began stealing from other residents, fighting with residents and staff, truanting from school and involving himself in illegal activity. He finally absconded from this facility."

When the man arrived in prison he boasted to staff that he "had many disciplinary reports during his last [prison] sentence, including several fights resulting in keeplock." He also announced that "if he has any problem with other inmates he will not go to the 'police' but will handle it himself." The man later proved as good as his word and had to be transferred to an adult prison. Here he rejected treatment, insisting he had no drug problem.

The man's status as an established career offender was thus cemented. His chances were assessed by a probation officer after his last robbery:

> The defendant's actions in the instant offense reflect the defendant's desire to remain active in a criminally deviant subculture involved in both drugs and strong-arm robbery. . . . Furthermore, the

defendant's prior legal history and his actions in the instant offense are almost identical in that his actions were crimes perpetrated on the city streets aimed at unassuming and innocent individuals. . . . While on parole supervision, the defendant managed to be arrested on two separate occasions. . . . The defendant's actions in the instant offense are relevant to his past criminal behavior, and despite the defendant's youth, reflect behavior consistent with that of a habitual offender.

Late Career Robbers

Our third robbery cluster contains older robbers who have long-term violence experience and extensive criminal histories. Most of the group have prison records, and many (44 percent) are nominally under supervision when they reoffend. However, the violence the offenders commit late in life is often less serious than that of young robbers, including themselves when young.

The members of the group often have long-term difficulties. One offender's career was summarized at prison intake as "a long history from childhood of social maladjustment, fighting and violent criminal offenses that are following him to adulthood." The criminal career referred to had begun at age ten, when the offender participated in his first recorded robbery. Earlier, the man's mother had been subject to a neglect petition, to which she responded that her son was "the most maladjusted and disruptive child in the neighborhood."

The man absconded from the juvenile facility in which he was placed, incurred thirteen arrests (for burglary, robbery, and larceny) before he qualified as an adult and graduated to a reformatory. Later the man specialized in stickups in which he threatened his victims with a gun. In his last offense he robbed a cabdriver, evicted him from his cab, and led police on a high-speed chase.

The man's third prison sentence was a long one. After an unpromising start the man—who when he had left school was reading at a second-grade level—graduated from junior college, applied to a drug program, and cemented his relationship with his son, suggesting that there had been a possible turnabout in his career.

Another late-maturing career is that of a man whose first offense was a serious assault on a female victim. The man later became involved in rapes, robberies, and combinations of rape and robbery. In one incident he and a fellow sadist placed a bag over a woman's head and raped and robbed her. On another occasion the man threatened, beat, raped, and robbed a neighbor, ostensibly because of money she owed him.

The man's last offense was a more conventional robbery, in which he carried a gun. His prison sentence was long because he was also convicted of having jumped bail, and he decided to enroll in a prison program designed to rehabilitate violence-prone persons. In addition he took a vocational course, in which he performed creditably.

The cluster heading under which these men fall describes offenders in the late stages of their career. This means that violence deescalation may occur, and career desistance is possible.

Violence Generalists

Our last category consists of offenders who engage in variegated serious violence. They have dense arrest histories and long-term violence problems. Some (25 percent) are mentally deficient, and others (32 percent) are intoxicated when they commit crimes.

The group combines attributes of exploders and robbers. Its violent offenses are often felony-related but at the same time, or at other times, are irrational and impulse-ridden.

Some members of the group have substance abuse problems. A case in point is that of an offender who was an alcoholic and also a drug addict and mentally retarded. A psychiatrist in the prison speculated about the link between the man's problems. He commented, "[This offender] probably had difficulties coping with the environmental requirements and as a result, he was seeking refuge in alcohol and cocaine in order to overcome his insecurity and anxieties."

In turn, alcohol had created more problems for the offender. He developed a penchant for drunk driving, which included running over police in an effort to escape. He had also attempted a robbery in which he assaulted his victim. In a third incident, he shot at a school full of children and explained that "I had nothing better to do at the time." The police to whom he delivered this account concluded that "the defendant was under the influence of alcohol at arrest" and that he was dangerous.

Another alcohol-involved offender had a barroom argument and slashed a woman in the abdomen, causing very serious injuries. The man had a long criminal record, including convictions for assault, burglary, robbery, larceny, resisting arrest, and ringing false fire alarms. At prison entry, he was described as "a predicate felon, if not a persistent felon." He in turn informed prison staff that he wanted "individual counseling in order to better understand himself with the hope of not returning to prison."

Members of the generalist cluster are often candidates for services—such as substance abuse services—which they have not received. The omission makes the offenders "nondisturbed" (because mental health status hinges on services received) and draws attention to other attributes they share. Unfortunately these attributes are chronicity and a penchant for violence, which evoke images of predatory careers, though the offenders are fringe figures whose careers are really only haphazard collages of frequently impulse-ridden involvements.

The Mental Health Continuum

A reader might well conclude that differences between offenders who have mental health histories and those who lack such histories are not striking. This impression would not rest on the suspicion that disturbed offenders are unfairly stigmatized but on doubts about whether "nondisturbed" offenders earn many bills of mental health. Our vignettes (which are admittedly sparse) hint at careers of deprivation, deficits and nonresilience, addiction and self-destructiveness, impulsivity and perversity, heteronomy and explosiveness. In this respect, the accounts are no different from the range of histories covered in thousands of presentence summaries the reader might peruse elsewhere.

Few offenders we described seem to be models of mental wellness as most of us would understand the phrase. These "nondisturbed" offenders are not sturdy professionals competently engaged in illegal occupations. They are not persons who resolutely elect unfortunate sources of income or drastic solutions to their problems. Many of these offenders have long-term "careers," but they drift, seemingly helplessly, from one juncture to the next. Even when the offenders' crimes are substantial, the perpetrators are often limited and driven, or exude incompetence and marginality.

That is not to say that the offenders we describe can be classed as disturbed, but that they are not mentally healthy. This means that they are not likely to receive help as long as mental health services subserve (as they do) the "medical model," which targets attention to diagnosed maladies—a far cry from promoting health. Persons who fall in the definitional penumbra (nonhealthy–nondisturbed) fall between the cracks of "health professions" that have become "illness professions" in practice.

What makes the situation ironic for offenders is that proposals to incorporate a more salient concern with mental health (that is, with personal effectiveness or coping competence) in correctional settings invite objections on the grounds that most offenders are nondisturbed, which makes the medical model inapplicable. Treatment will thus continue to be constrained until we entertain the unfashionable notions that (1) a continuum exists from (mental) illness to health, and that (2) movement along the continuum from mental illness toward mental health can be a goal of intervention.

Chapter 7

The Disturbed Violent Offense

The study of offenders who have emotional problems differs from the description of offenses that are affected by emotional problems. Like other behavior, a violent crime can be a symptom of a person's psychological difficulties, but disturbed persons are often capable of committing offenses that are indistinguishable from those perpetrated by nondisturbed offenders. The other side of the coin is that many offenses of ostensibly sturdy offenders can reflect nonsturdy motives such as loss of control or impulsivity.

Both of these facts are compatible with contemporary thinking which rejects the notions that (1) violence and irrationality are the monopoly of a group of people who are different from the rest of us, and that (2) illness/normalcy and crime/law-abidingness represent dichotomous behavior. The first point is emphasized by a report from a Violence Commission task force, which notes,

> A popular view of psychoanalytic and psychiatric theories is that they explain why "crazy" people behave as they do. While specialists in these fields do work most often with disturbed people, they also have a general view of life in which antisocial behavior is always present, either in potential or actual form. At the same time, they seek

to understand the special role that violent behavior may serve for people who are deeply sick–or at least sicker than others.[1]

The second point is underlined by—among others—Seymour Halleck, who writes, "Most modern psychiatrists look upon mental illness as a process. Mental health and mental illness are both viewed on the same continuum. The behavior of some individuals may at times become so ineffective, so self-punitive or so irrational that the psychiatrist deems it advisable to define them as ill."[2] In another passage Halleck suggests that crimes and symptoms may be interchangeable variations on maladaptive behavior, which means that "the same individual may show symptoms of schizophrenia on one day and of obsessive preoccupation on the next. On the third day he might commit a crime, and on the fourth he might be entirely docile and comfortable."[3]

The point implied by such statements is that any segment of behavior can be examined independently of the judgments we make about the behaving person, though once we have enough of a person's conduct to assess we can describe behavioral trends involving change or consistency. Halleck also implies that the labeling of behavior as disturbed does not require exotic expertise in that "ultimately, most of our decisions to call people mentally ill are based upon judgments of reasonableness."[4] An offender who commits a professional robbery, for example, is mostly viewed as a "rational" offender, because "it is assumed that the criminal is seeking goals that everyone can understand and accept, goals such as financial profit or status."[5] If the same person attempts to commit robberies while he is drunk, our assessment may become more reserved, on the grounds that "a reasonable man would not undertake a difficult criminal task while intoxicated. If he must depend upon crime to earn his living, he is behaving no more

1. D. J. Mulvihill and M. M. Tumin, with L. A. Curtis, eds., *Crimes of Violence. A Staff Report to the National Commission on the Causes and Prevention of Violence* (Washington, D.C.: Government Printing Office, 1969), 12:459.

2. S. L. Halleck, *Psychiatry and the Dilemmas of Crime* (New York: Harper and Row, 1969), 40.

3. Ibid.

4. Ibid., 47.

5. Ibid., 48.

reasonably than a surgeon who would try to operate while inebriated."[6]

Such ratings of the "reasonableness" of specific crimes need not imply, of course, that the offenders are reasonable or unreasonable. But it should be obvious that offenses can be psychologically revealing acts to the extent that they are shaped by the goals and concerns of individual offenders, reflecting their skills and deficits, including intellectual, emotional, and social deficits. Where deficits are substantial, one expects that crimes will be contaminated by them, sometimes subtly and sometimes dramatically and blatantly. Should this occur, the sum of many "unreasonable" offenses approximates a composite disturbed perpetrator:

> When the criminal fails to pursue acceptable goals in a logical, consistent or effective manner, we must assume either that he is inept at solving ordinary problems, that he has met with environmental circumstances which he cannot master, or that he is driven by motivations which are not apparent and which deviate from those which society would consider reasonable. These are all qualities that could just as easily describe the mentally ill. We, therefore, must return to our earlier assertion that if the judgments by which we designate unreasonable behavior were consistently applied to the law violator, we would have to agree that many criminals behave in a manner that is not too dissimilar to that of the mentally ill.[7]

As it happens, our data permit us to explore the strategy of behavior-ratings that Halleck suggests. We can do so because we have concise descriptions of most offenses for which members of our samples were convicted. We also have an eccentricity code (described in chapter 2), which approximates Halleck's conception of "unreasonableness" in crime. This code lets us explore the range and quality of offenses that raise questions about the offender's mental state at the time of offending. The point is not to document the extent to which criminals are mentally disturbed, because statements about the prevalence of mental illness cannot be based on impressionistic judgments. The point, rather, is to

6. Ibid., 49.
7. Ibid.

venture hypotheses about the ways in which specialized dispositions of violent offenders (psychological problems) can affect
some of the offenses they commit.

Random Violence

The most uncontaminated relationship between violence and
emotional disorders exists in incidents in which strangers are
assaulted without provocation and seemingly at random. Such
violence is most apt to be perpetrated by Disturbed Exploders
and has repercussions that transcend its numerical importance.
This is so because victims have no way of predicting or preventing
victimization when offenders offer no cue to their impending
resolve and strike out of the blue. Random violence also makes
disturbed persons in general objects of fear, since it is the sort of
violence that is exclusive to (though unrepresentative of) pathologically tinged offenses.

The reason random violence can without exception be ascribed to serious mental disorders is that its inception is invariably
associated with psychotic delusions or hallucinations. The offense
may appear motiveless, since the offender usually assigns private,
symbolic attributes to victims who happen to be available at the
time the offender's delusions or hallucinations reach climactic
junctures. To the extent to which external stimuli play a role in
provoking the offender's violent act, the role is always bizarre and
improbable, one in which the victim becomes a repository of
grievances the offender derives elsewhere. An illustration of this
sequence is provided by the following scenario:

> The offender—a man in his midthirties—paces a subway platform
> mouthing the words "push, push, push," scanning his surroundings
> in what is described as "a nervous manner." The offender then ap-
> proaches a young Oriental woman waiting for a train and pushes her
> under an incoming engine, which crushes and decapitates her. The
> offender is overheard saying, "Now we're even. I did it. Now they'll
> see at school." After being arrested, the man has a telephone conver-
> sation with his sister in which he explains, "This is not my fault. It is
> the Board of Education."

The antecedent sequence in this incident was that the offender
had been a teacher and was placed on medical leave after experi-

encing the onset of a schizophrenic condition. He was hospitalized and treated as an outpatient but discontinued his therapy and medication against the advice of his physicians. He then returned to his job, but his performance proved substandard, and he received letters of admonition from his principal. The resulting anxiety contributed to a resurgence of the man's psychosis, which now centered on a delusional system which made him the target of a conspiracy. On the day of his offense the man had had lunch at a Chinese restaurant, and the waiter asked him what he did for a living. This question led the man to conclude that the Chinese community was in league with his superiors, who were the source of his difficulties. He also concluded that the Chinese as a group were "interfering with his mind and poisoning him to make him homosexual."

A second offender who attempted (unsuccessfully) to throw a stranger under an incoming subway train had spent "90 percent of twenty years" in psychiatric settings. In this instance, psychological difficulties had a remote origin and dated to the man's military service decades earlier. The man's behavior included angry outbursts and actions that were irrationally impulsive. He could offer no reason for committing his offense, and after he was incarcerated the prison intake analyst observed that "in every way he is an institutionalized psychiatric patient who belongs in a hospital rather than a prison."

Personal experiences that precipitate random violence can generalize from one target to another in psychological chain reactions. A case in point is that of a female patient who had been living on the street. One month previously this patient had been raped, and she had acquired a screwdriver to "defend herself." She had also become obsessed with delusions revolving around birth and maternity concerns, which culminated in a random attack on an infant in a stroller. The child's mother fought off the incursion, but in the course of the melee the patient turned her attention to an elderly bystander, whom she stabbed with her screwdriver.

Another chronic outpatient became involved in the following sequence:

> The patient walks the streets in an agitated state, mumbling to himself. A pedestrian asks him whether anything is the matter, and in

response he pulls a knife and stabs the pedestrian in the face. By this time a crowd has gathered and the offender slashes two of the bystanders. The police arrive, and the man menaces one of the officers with a knife and is shot in the leg.

In another example,

The offender walks up to a stranger on the street, grabs him and cuts his throat and chin. He subsequently explains that "his friend, with whom he had worked, had died of cancer. He felt that two other people would die. He was suspicious that he was being attacked."

In other incidents the offender's concerns have more focus, in that they attach to a particular individual who triggers a specific obsession. Examples include the following:

The offender enters a laundromat armed with a knife and encounters a stranger. The stranger leaves the laundromat and is followed by the offender, who stabs him in the back and throws bottles at him. The offender tells the victim, "I'll kill you if I see you [again] on this street."

The offender peeks through a window and sees a woman taking a shower. He enters the house, picks up a knife and knives the victim in the arm, neck and back, subsequently indicating he has "no idea why" he committed the offense.

In some instances delusional concerns center on the offender's perceptions of the victim's behavior, and the violence becomes quasi random rather than random. This means that the victim has at some point dealt with the offender, but that the connotations the offender assigns to the victim's acts are improbable and bizarre, and thus unpredictable. An example is the following chain of events:

Two days prior to his violent crime the offender has gone to a welfare office to inquire about his check. The caseworker is not in the office and the offender leaves a message. On the day of the offense the offender returns and wordlessly stabs his caseworker with an icepick. He explains, "I had to get my rent paid. I was afraid I would be thrown out of my place. [If I had used my hands instead of the weapon] I would probably have to go back there over and over again to see about my check."

Another example involves a disturbed female parolee who

knifes a woman in a washroom, explaining that "the victim bumped into me and didn't apologize."

Most random violence one encounters is an uncontaminated product of delusions and bizarre impulses, but some random violence (though not an appreciable proportion) includes some contribution of alcohol and/or drugs to the offender's explosive state of mind at the time of the offense. The following examples are cases in point:

> The offender runs up to a woman who is waiting for a bus, and hits her in the face with a tree limb, breaking her nose; the woman falls, and the offender continues to assault her. He then "vigorously resists" arrest and police conclude that he "is high on angel dust."

> The offender has been drinking heavily in a tavern, exits and points a crossbow at passersby, two off-duty police officers intercede, and the offender stabs them.

Not surprisingly, offenders who commit random violence often hypothesize that motives for their behavior are unascertainable. The offenders' inability to "explain" their violence relates to their confusion and agitation at the time of their explosions—which cannot be recaptured in retrospect—but also has to do with the complexity of motives that underlie random violence. We have noted that more than other violence, random violence is a product of delusions or hallucinations. This means that the motives for the violence are related to the dynamics of the offender's emotional difficulties, including their long-term developmental origins. Such relationships must at best be inferred, as in classic examples in which sex-related anxieties lead to panic which is ascribed (via delusions) to external danger. The instances in which offenders themselves can pinpoint such dynamics are rare. On occasions this identification occurs, however, as in the following incident:

> The offender—who is a transvestite—drives his car through a red light. When he is flagged down by police, he speeds away, and crashes into a wall. Approached by the police he exits his car, swinging a knife, shouting, "I'll kill you. Kill me!" The offender indicates that at the time he is "extremely upset over his masculinity," and has been suffering bouts of depression. He recalls that when his car crashed "he truly hoped the police would kill him."

Arson and Emotional Disturbance

A second category of violence that is almost always associated with emotional problems is incendiary violence or criminal arson, which is most often perpetrated by Disturbed Sex Offenders, Compensatory Offenders, and Skid Row Exploders. The dynamics of arson offenses are variegated and are insufficiently understood, but some offenses shed light on prevalent motivational patterns. One such pattern combines impulsivity, impotent rage, and a sense of lingering resentment. The following examples are cases in point:

> While walking by a house in an intoxicated state the offender remembers an altercation with the owner of the house that occurred several years previously. Inspired by this recollection, the offender smashes a bowling ball through the victim's car window, pours gasoline through the window, and sets the automobile on fire.

> The offender—whose intelligence is extremely limited—has done work for his landlord in exchange for promised compensation. Instead of a reasonable wage, the landlord pays the offender a very small sum (four dollars). The offender feels resentful, gets drunk, and starts a fire in his closet. He also sets fire to his apartment on another occasion after fortifying himself with alcohol. On this date he has not received a promised food donation and has discovered that a neighbor to whom he feels attached "does not like him."

> The offender, who is drunk, sets fire to an apartment building, doing minor damage to the building's garage. The offender reports that the owner has called her "names." She indicates that she has reported the affront to the police, who "refused to do anything."

> Another offender has set five fires, resulting in damage of $300,000. One fire destroys the garage in the offender's father's house. The offender reports disagreements with his father. After these acrimonious arguments, he testifies, he gets drunk and sets fires.

> The offender, while intoxicated, incinerates a bedroom to injure her sleeping husband, with whom she has had an argument.

In incidents such as these one factor we invariably encounter is the offender's feeling that he or she is overwhelmed or resourceless in conflicts with opponents who are powerful. This suggests that the offender has a low level of self-esteem and a limited sense of self-efficacy. Another denominator that cuts across the incidents is that the offender drinks alcohol as a precondition to firesetting to work up his or her resolve.

Though resentment and a sense of impotence are a frequent motive for arson, some more complex patterns are detailed by a few offenders. One ambiguous account, for example, emerges in the following incident:

> The offender—who suffers from retardation—has set two fires in a motel that do extensive damage. He is a former employee who had been recently discharged, but claims, "I had nothing against the motel . . . without thinking I would just go and light a fire anywhere." The man explains that he sets fires in response to hallucinations in which he sees the face of an individual who has killed his sister, and that he sets the fires to "get even" and to reduce tension he feels; "then everything builds up and I do it over again."

As it happens, the offender's account is incomplete, in that his fire-setting proves to be a long-term pattern. The offender had set several fires preceding the incident (his sister's death) which he regards as catalytic. This fact is not surprising, however, in that predispositions to arson are often chronic, while specific stimuli (such as feeling rejected) enter as shorter-term, reinforcing motives.

It is also not surprising that arsonists attribute their offenses to immediate antecedents, since longer-term motives are hard (if not impossible) to characterize. This difficulty contributes to the fact that arsonists' self-descriptions often include claims to rational, goal-directed, or calculated behavior. The following incidents are illustrative:

> The offender breaks into a construction office to "look around" and steals a pen from a desk. He decides to "cover up finger prints" to avoid capture by strewing flammable liquid over the office, burning it down and causing several million dollars' worth of damage.

> The offender has been rejected by a female friend and sets her house on fire. He claims he has done so to "play the hero" by rescuing his friend's children, thereby inspiring her to renew their liaison.

Some offenders react to the difficulty of trying to explain their irrational acts by attributing their offenses to intoxication ("when

I drink I set fires") or highlighting the enjoyment they derive from watching fires after they are set. Both observations are relevant, but neither gives adequate weight to longer-term motivational states documented by the mental health histories of arsonists.

Mental Health Problems and Retaliatory Violence

Retaliatory violence is committed by a wide range of people, including persons who have no criminal histories, those who have extensive involvements with violence, and those with emotional problems, substance abuse difficulties, and cognitive disabilities.

There is no distinguishably different pattern of "crazy retaliation," but some retaliatory violence resembles quasi-random violence (for example, a man cuts a person's face repeatedly for throwing a snowball at him); other incidents can combine retaliatory motives with concerns that are in fact symptoms of mental illness (for example, a man kills his wife after having an argument with her and hearing voices that tell him to kill her). In other instances the motives for the violence are contaminated by eccentric overtones or implausible premises that run through explanations of offenses, as in the following examples:

> The offender—who has been hospitalized on occasion for treatment of schizophrenia—engages in arguments with her fiance two days before her wedding. During the course of these arguments, she stabs her fiance to death, and later explains that she "was choked to death by light-complected members of the black race who had joined in a conspiracy to destroy her via [the boyfriend's] death." She also claims that the police has substituted the murder weapon for a "dagger" brandished by the victim.

> A man kills his brother-in-law with a twelve-gauge shotgun, calls his sister [the victim's wife] and asks her "to clean up the mess." He claims the victim has sexually molested his two daughters and "taunted him about performing sexual acts with him." He complains that he has shared such concerns with relatives, but "no one would believe him."

Retaliatory offenses are responses to perceived affronts, but it is not uncommon for disturbed retaliators to add unusual twists to standard acts of retribution, which include inappropriate and highly unusual behavior during or after the offense:

> The offender suspects that his wife is involved in extramarital liaisons. He stabs the sleeping wife in the neck, then chokes her with a telephone cord. The police find the offender "dazed" and describe him as "incoherent."

> The victim is the offender's ex-girlfriend, whom he has harassed "in order to get her back." In the incident the offender takes a shotgun and holds the girl for sixteen hours "trying to get up the courage to kill himself in front of her." He uses the gun, shooting out windows, before giving himself up to the police.

> The offender is a homosexual, and is also retarded. The victim is the man's lover, who has provoked him by becoming attentive to another man. The offender stabs his lover in the back, eats dinner and asks a neighbor to call the police, who find the victim dead.

The irrational extreme among acts of retaliation is behavior involving disinhibited (angry, explosive) overkill, including massive, disproportionate rage in response to seemingly minor provocations. Explosions of unrestrained rage are not confined to any special group of offenders. Among some alcoholics, however— most notably, Skid Row Exploders—carefree, indiscriminate expressions of anger suggest a contribution of alcohol to the genesis of retaliatory resolves. Examples of disinhibiting alcohol involvement include the following acts of revenge:

> The offender has been "drinking excessively." A police officer finds him blocking the exit to a bus terminal and asks him to move. The offender responds, "You're done, motherfucker," and attempts to shoot the officer with his service revolver.

> The offender is a supervisor in a rooming house. While intoxicated, he encounters a nonresident using a bathroom without permission. He arms himself with a baseball bat, waits for the victim to exit, and beats him to death.

> The offender assaults a fellow patron in a bar, kicks and beats two female police officers who try to restrain him, and assaults a male officer, kicking him in the groin. After the man is nominally subdued and taken to a hospital, he assaults doctors and nurses by spitting at them.

> The offender is a chronic schizophrenic who has been described as

a man who "becomes paranoid and wanders aimlessly about." He has been drinking with the victim in the latter's apartment. The victim asks him to leave, and the offender stabs the man in the heart.

Drug disinhibition (notably that of PCP and cocaine) is also sometimes associated with acts of retaliatory overkill, and there are also instances in which the effects of drug and alcohol disinhibition seem to occur in combination:

> After an argument, the offender kills the victim, striking him with blunt instruments and then strangling him to death. The offender "states he was drinking and smoking angel dust, and does not remember the incident."

> The offender has a fight with an elderly drinking companion over a bottle of wine. During the fight, he stabs, punches and chokes the victim in such a frenzy that others cannot stop him. He claims to have been drunk and "high on PCP."

The most dramatic disinhibition occurs among offenders whose violence has a tantrumlike flavor. In such violence the offender appears to run helplessly out of control and can do a great deal of harm, as in the following incident:

> The offender injures an acquaintance after an argument. He also injures police officers who try to arrest him, lifting them and "banging them against a wall." A repeat performance occurs in the prison, during which four officers try to subdue the offender and are seriously injured. Prison staff note that "it seems that [the offender's] size and occasional episodes of dull-witted behavior may make him look like an easy target for others to pick on to prove themselves, although, due to his mental state, he is also capable of misinterpreting others' intentions and reacting explosively without real provocation.

The offender in this example reliably inflicts damage because he is large and throws repeat tantrums. The man's size is an unusual and unique attribute, but the combination of chronicity and promiscuous explosiveness occurs elsewhere among offenders with mental health histories. The following are some cases in point that involve recurrent and redundant explosions:

> The offender's difficulties include early referrals for "uncontrollable temper tantrums," including breaking a teacher's fingers and "destroying property at school." In the most recent incident he shoots

at a man he has previously stabbed, against whom he harbors a "grudge." He has also thrown a knife at a sister (puncturing her leg), threatened to kill his brother and grandmother, and "sexually attacked" a female acquaintance.

The offender has spent six years in a psychiatric hospital. He is imprisoned for explosions in which he (1) stabs a former girlfriend's new boyfriend; (2) blinds the girlfriend by stabbing her in the face, and (3) beats up the girl's father, threatening to burn down his house. In prison the man remains assaultive, "admits having no control over his explosive nature and does not care what he does to others."

In jail, the offender, who is awaiting trial for an assault, attacks a corrections officer because his shampoo is missing, throws hot water in the face of an inmate with whom he has argued, and injures two officers who try to restrain him.

The offenders involved in these incidents have histories of diagnosed difficulties, but explosive violence also occurs among men and women who have no such histories, most notably among Patterned Exploders. A propensity to disinhibition—the tendency to allow oneself to explode under stress—draws attention to the contributing role of reality-obfuscating factors we have referred to, which may be external (alcohol and drugs) and/or internal states. The latter are obviously important and include emotional lability and cognitive dysfunctions which impair appraisals of threat or assessments of response options.

Vehicular Violence

Among unusual forms of violence which reflect the influence of disinhibition are some extreme violent assaults in which cars are used as weapons. Serious vehicular violence can involve destructive impulsivity, panic, and indifference to consequences (including one's personal survival). Though such violence often features alcohol as an impairing influence, it also provides a role for other disinhibitors, such as those associated with emotional problems.

Vehicular violence by disturbed offenders includes serious incidents such as the following:

The offender has tried to break into his inlaws' home. When police arrive, the offender backs a stolen car into three officers, then attempts to escape on foot. One officer sustains a hip and a head injury when the car is backed into him. Another officer is dragged a hundred feet down the street. The offender explains that he has arrived to talk to his wife, who he thinks has died in a plane crash. He is also there to see a friend from Venus, who has returned to help with his problems, and feels the police have interrupted his colloquy with his extraterrestrial friend.

The offender has a history of assaulting police officers and prison guards. Preceding his offense he has been ordered to stop his car. He speeds away but later returns, taps the officer on the shoulder, and asks him whether he has a problem. He locks himself in his car, and when ordered to exit drives the car into the officer, into a parked car, and into a police vehicle that responds to the scene.

The offender is a disturbed juvenile escapee. He steals a pocketbook and is intercepted by a witness as he steals a van. He drives over the witness and drags him down the street, killing him. He explains that "I got crazy the way things were going."

These incidents show admixtures of confusion, anger, and fear. The same ingredients characterize more conventional incidents, but (1) the break with reality may be less drastic than it is among some disturbed offenders, and (2) the role of alcohol may make the contribution of psychological problems the offenders may have less salient:

The offender is a former mental patient who lives in a trailer park. He is intoxicated and announces that he is going shopping, but a neighbor prevents him from driving off. The offender then agrees to go to bed, but later changes his mind, threatening his neighbor (offering to burn down his trailer) if he does not relinquish his ignition keys. He drives out with tires spinning, kills a pedestrian, and announces that he is leaving town to avoid "going to jail for life this time."

The offender accuses a man of stealing from his girlfriend, drives over the man repeatedly, then aims his car at the girlfriend, who he alleges has been "paying too much attention" to the victim.

One motive which may at some level form part of disinhibiting sequences involving the use of automobiles is indifference to survival, but the role of this factor (which at minimum consists of a cavalier disregard of danger to oneself) is purely a subject for speculation, as it is for more conventional DWI offenses, in which no victimization is intended.

Sexual Violence

Persons with mental health or substance abuse histories are over-represented among offenders who commit sexual assaults against adults or (more so) against children. This statistical fact confirms that deep-seated dispositions figure among routine motives for rape and sodomy and that sexual violence is often complex in its dynamics. In view of this observation it is not surprising that sexual violence is frequently recidivistic as well as impervious to deterrence through imprisonment, though relatively few disturbed sex offenders have experienced prison. Adding to the seriousness of this picture is the fact that victims of sexual violence are frequently depersonalized and callously dealt with by offenders whose obsessiveness and incapacity for empathy is extreme. Victims in such offenses are responded to as objects of need-satisfaction, and in the most serious incidents are treated with quasi-sadistic disregard for their physical survival:

> An offender abducts a twelve-year-old girl, rapes and sodomizes her, and leaves her zippered in a suitcase.

> An offender abducts a woman at a party, rapes and beats her and leaves her under subzero conditions in which she narrowly survives.

> The offender rapes a mother and beats and kicks her four-year-old daughter.

> The offender rapes a deaf-mute girl, who must be hospitalized as a result of serious injuries.

> The offender sodomizes a seven-year-old boy at knife point, urinates in his mouth, and leaves him covered with abrasions.

> The offender attacks a patient suffering from cerebral palsy, abandons him in freezing weather, and steals his wheelchair. His comment to the victim (who almost dies) is, "Good-bye, sucker."

Offenses such as forcible rapes of infants and assaults on persons of advanced age are predations in which victims can be preselected for their helplessness as well as for their implausibility as sexual targets. Additional pathological nuances sometimes manifest themselves in the details of unfolding incidents, such as in the following examples:

> The offender enters the victims' apartment, knifes the husband and tries to rape the wife. When police arrive he throws a bottle at

them, and tells them they cannot arrest him without a warrant. The man's blood alcohol is .16; he has convulsions and must be taken to a hospital.

The offender forces his way into an occupied apartment, complains that it is a pigsty, and makes the occupant wash dishes. He then kisses her, watching himself in a mirror, and explains to her that everyone gets raped, including himself in jail. He then rapes the victim and tells her that he will drown her in her bathtub.

The offender abducts a pedestrian and tries to rape her. He explains that (1) he is intoxicated, and (2) has heard voices instructing him to have intercourse with a woman.

Students of abnormal behavior assume that some sexual assaults—particularly of children and other powerless victims—are compensatory efforts by persons who feel (and often are) inadequate. In this view, men who are afraid to approach adult partners can gain sexual satisfaction and forceful dominance against helpless—and therefore nonthreatening—targets. The generality of this explanation is in some dispute, but illustrative documentation of inadequacy includes incidents such as the following:

The victim is intoxicated, is sleeping soundly in the subway, and remains asleep while the offense takes place. The offender (a mental patient) subjects the victim to oral sex while another man (not associated with the offender) tries to rape her.

The offender exposes himself to an elderly lady, takes off some of her clothes, and flees. The next day the victim sees the offender in front of her home, where he hangs out, and he is arrested.

The offender is a mentally defective outpatient who partially disrobes a female pedestrian, but is subdued by other pedestrians before he can attempt to rape her.

Mismanaged Offenses

Offenders who appear limited or disturbed at the time of their offenses, such as many Acute Disturbed Exploders and Compensatory Offenders, can have their efficacy as crime perpetrators reduced.[8] Though the proportion of disturbed persons who fail

8. Charles E. Silberman points out that bungled offenses are a testimonial to the spontaneity and lack of planning with which many offenders approach their

as career criminals is surprisingly small (which suggests that crime is not an occupation calling for sophisticated skills), some persons are clearly too impaired to function effectively in carrying out specific offenses. Among instances of failure due to impairment are robberies in which offenders try to follow standard robbery procedures but become unconvincing because of their obvious instability or eccentricity:

> The offender gives a supermarket cashier a note that says, "I don't mind dying; you'll go with me if you don't give me a stack of twenties and fifties." The cashier cannot open her register due to nervousness. The offender takes his note and leaves the store. He is promptly overtaken and arrested.

> The offender approaches a subway booth he has robbed, apologizes to the attendant, and tells her he is going to mug someone. He does and is arrested.

> The offender robs a gas station. He is recognized because he has been in the station before and has filled out employment applications listing his name and address. He is described by the victim as "very nervous" at the time of the offense.

> The offender enters a gas station wielding a knife and announces, "This is a stickup." The owner and two sons respond, "You've got to be kidding." As they subdue the offender, he yells, "I am an officer; call the police. I'm a detective." The police arrive and arrest him.

> The offender enters a bank claiming to have a bomb, demanding money. The teller laughs at the offender and he flees. A short time later he jumps over the counter, takes money, and is arrested. He claims to have no recollection of the incident, since he was under the influence of alcohol and drugs.

> The offender tries to rob different banks using deposit slips of other banks and is informed that he is "in the wrong bank." He eventually does rob a bank and leaves a deposit slip with his name on it.

In incidents such as these, the offender's failure as a criminal can arise from (1) ambivalence or lack of self-confidence, (2) inap-

---

vocation. He suggests further that such offenses are partly responsible for the fact that clearance rates (which for some offense categories are low) do not describe the probability of being arrested (which for repeat offenders is high). See *Criminal Violence, Criminal Justice* (New York: Random House, Vintage Books, 1980).

propriate behavior which reduces the credibility of his threats, and/or (3) self-destructive behavior which increases the probability of capture. Similar traits can reduce the efficacy of residential burglaries, as in the following examples:

> The offender has spent his paycheck on a drinking binge. He enters an apartment but flees when the occupant wakes up. He enters a second apartment and again wakes up the occupant, who steps on him as he tries to hide. He tries to flee but is grabbed by the occupant of the first apartment, who finds him "in a daze."

> The offender talks to an answering machine of a former employer indicating that he is going to burglarize the man. He does and is arrested.

> The offender burglarizes a home and lingers to take a shower. He burglarizes a second house and lies on a lounge chair on the porch, where a neighbor observes him and calls the police.

> The offender's IQ is 55. He burglarizes an apartment leaving behind his shoes and his wallet, later explaining that he was intoxicated.

> The offender breaks into an unoccupied apartment and steals property, but abandons his hat and jacket. He also leaves feces on the floor.

In incidents such as these, the perpetrator shows that he lacks the capacity to complete an offense without risking apprehension. In other instances, offenses are undertaken on the spur of the moment (for example, the offender drinks and runs out of money, crosses the street to rob a bank, and returns to resume drinking), and they thus qualify as clumsy expressions of half-baked impulsivity rather than as manifestations of resolve, planning, or "criminal intent."

Violence Overkill in Burglaries and Robberies

Very different from self-destructive inadequacy is the use of gratuitous violence in committing property-related violent offenses. Offenders with mental health histories are less prone than offenders without such histories to commit violent property offenses, but they are more likely to use excessive violence when they do commit such offenses. This fact is hardly surprising because violence overkill is not a "rational" way to conduct criminal business, in that it is unnecessary to achieve the ostensible goal (monetary gain) of the offense.

Extreme violence among disturbed offenders can express long-term traits (such as a disposition to casually take life) or shorter-term situational motives (such as blind excitation or rage). Compounded irrationality can increase the sadistic flavor of violence, such as in the following incidents:

> The offender robs a gas station, then takes the attendant into the woods and stabs him with a machete, breaks his arms and legs, and slashes his neck and chest, leaving him for dead. In a previous offense he has locked a cabdriver into the trunk of his cab and abandoned the cab, which is not found until four days later. The offender is a mental patient and a member of a satanic cult who "from adolescence has been a bizarre, violent, warped sadomasochist," who declares that he "is not afraid to die nor eliminate anyone who antagonizes him."

> The offender participates in the robbery of a fast food establishment. After the robbery, he goes into the store and shoots the manager in the head. He tells a cabdriver he has kidnapped, "I had to shoot that motherfucker. . . . Twenty-five years don't mean nothin' to me. No one wants me anyway. I'll shoot you too."

> The offender robs four stores. In the first, he shoots the owner three times in the head. He shoots his other victims in the chest, killing one of them. He is a chronic outpatient who has no criminal record and claims no recall of the offenses.

> The offender enters the home of a paralyzed veteran, dragging him from room to room and beating him. He keeps beating his victim because he is "infuriated" that the man has no money.

> The offender enters a house, steals property, then shoots and kills the family pets—a retriever and a ferret. He testifies that "he remembers little of that day as he had been drinking heavily and had taken PCP."

> The offender beats an elderly woman with a cane and kicks her in the face while mugging her. He is a disturbed transvestite with a history of robbing older, defenseless women.

> The offender throws his victim against a wall and demands money, and the victim hands over his wallet. The offender removes money

and then demands the victim's shoes and jacket. Thereafter he tries to strangle the victim, throws him down a flight of stairs and kicks him in the head. He explains that he is "high on angel dust."

Some offenders mention drugs as contributing to their readiness to use gratuitous violence, but patients with drug histories are underrepresented in the more extreme felony violence incidents. This suggests that drug-caused excitation is mostly not the only causal factor at work. To the extent to which drugs and emotional problems combine to spark violence overkill, mood enhancers (such as angel dust) may simply reinforce preexistent violent dispositions.

Extreme felony violence is not a psychotic symptom, in the sense that it is not behavior that responds to command hallucinations or delusions. If a common motivational denominator exists, it is an effort to demonstrate power through one's ability to maim or kill. Victims trigger the violence by being helpless, which makes them easy, inviting proving grounds for the toughness the offender senses that he lacks. One cue is that cruelty often coexists with self-destructive behavior, including suicide attempts, and periodic despondency. This paradox derives from the offender's view of the world as a dog-eat-dog place in which one is alternatively a victim and a victimizer. The offender is also typically tense, highstrung, and irritable and full of bitterness and pent up rage. This emotional state, combined with his outlook on life, creates his destructive disposition.

Chapter 8

The Extremely Disturbed but Minimally Violent Offender: The Problem of Sentencing

We shall recall (in chapter 9) that some offender subgroups are made up of chronically disturbed and very violent persons who are obvious candidates for imprisonment because they pose serious threats to society. Such persons tax prison resources and are at best warehoused in the prison, but they must be incapacitated for long periods to protect the community from extreme and unpredictably explosive conduct.

Other offenders are also disturbed but they pose lesser risk; more to the point, such offenders lack any "criminal intent" in the conventional sense of the term[1] and suffer from a variety of handicaps which create the adjustment problems under which much of their offense-related behavior can be subsumed. The need for incapacitation is not a pressing goal for such persons, the

1. Criminal intent (*mens rea*) literally means evil or guilty state of mind and refers to the "mental element" of any offense. Seymour Halleck, a forensic psychiatrist, notes that "in the modern era, our courts have rarely been concerned with the mental state of an offender as an exculpatory factor unless the state can be characterized as a disability sufficiently severe as to meet the legal standards defining insanity. The *mens rea* or mental element accompanying a crime has become narrowly defined, so that simple awareness of conduct, the circumstances under which it occurs, and its probable consequences are usually sufficient to assume intent or guilty mind" (Halleck, *The Mentally Disordered Offender*, 54).

probability of deterrence is usually negligible (since offenses are at best impulsive), and the concept of equitable punishment seems inapplicable, given that the harm that is done tends to be a corollary of clumsiness and confusion.

The type of disturbed offender who is not a public menace stands out unhappily as a prison inmate and tends to impress correctional staff as a victim of inappropriate, insensitive, or inhumane sentencing.

In a recent legislative hearing Commissioner Thomas Coughlin, the official in charge of New York prisons, expressed reservations about the disturbed and retarded offenders who are routinely sentenced to prison despite their obvious handicaps.[2] The commissioner advocated increased attention to this problem at the juncture of sentencing.

Coughlin said in part:

> Pre-trial identification of these individuals should be intensified. A number of mentally retarded inmates with abysmal coping skills have been tried, pled or convicted and sentenced to DOCS [the prison system's] custody. In some instances, these individuals were in non-correctional custodial care when the crime of conviction was committed. . . .
>
> As an agency, DOCS is not equipped to deal with these individuals. Although the most severe cases are few in number, they account for a disproportionate amount of staff intervention. Their presence in correctional facilities is highly disruptive to both staff and other inmates.
>
> Although [these offenders] have been adjudicated as being legally responsible for their actions, they function at an intellectual and social level well below that of the general inmate population.
>
> I would recommend that the lack of pre-trial services for developmentally disabled individuals be addressed by this committee. The current lack of such services is probably a contributing factor to the inappropriate incarceration of these individuals.[3]

2. Throughout this chapter we refer to *disturbed* offenders. Attention to our illustrations will remind us, however, that many of the inmates we discuss have multiple problems, combining (in varying degrees) serious retardation, learning deficits, and manifestations of mental illness.

3. Excerpts from the "Testimony of Commissioner Thomas A. Coughlin before the Assembly Standing Committees on Correction and Mental Health, Mental Retardation and Developmental Disabilities, December 9, 1987," *Public*

The Problem of Routine Sentencing

Our review of prison files confirmed that questions about the appropriateness of a prison sentence for the offender can be easily raised. Such questions particularly arise in situations in which (1) the offender is clearly not a menace to the public, (2) his or her offense is irrationally motivated and/or reflects the influence of serious disabilities, (3) the offender remains disturbed in the period following arrest and preceding trial, and (4) he or she continues disturbed at intake into the prison.

Examples of cases that meet these four criteria are not hard to locate, though the number of inmates involved is impossible to determine with precision, given that delicate judgments must be exercised and that information on which to base such judgments is often sparse. However, it is the nature of the problem, rather than its magnitude, that must be the first of our concerns.

What is the nature of the problem? It is that some inmates are *primarily* disturbed and *secondarily* offenders but have been disposed of as if they were primarily offenders and secondarily (if at all) disturbed. Such actions are not reprehensible because they deprive mentally ill persons of treatment, given that mental health services are available in prisons. The problem is rather that fragile individuals must now receive services in a setting that poses tough challenges to the limited coping capacities of non-resilient personalities.[4] This fact holds even when inmates must be hospitalized on one or more occasions, because hospitalization

---

Hearing on Persons with Developmental Disabilities and the Criminal Justice System. Coughlin advocates expansion of supportive services in the prison but recognizes that "in the short term, pressure [must] be put at the front end of the system, the courts, the prosecutors and the defense bar. Chronic schizophrenics with IQs of 67 should not be allowed to plead guilty and be sent to prison" (Coughlin, personal communication). The timeliness of Coughlin's testimony is illustrated by the fact that on the same date on which his remarks were publicized, a newspaper story appeared in which a county judge was quoted as objecting to procedures in the courts that allow "incapacitated persons to avoid criminal proceedings, [creating] a class of persons immune from the criminal justice system and given carte blanch [*sic*] to commit crime" (J. Cather, "Judge cites loopholes for mentally disturbed," Albany *Knickerbocker News,* December 10, 1987.

4. Mental health–related adjustment problems of inmates are discussed in Toch, *Men in Crisis.*

usually provides only a brief respite from prison life, and the commitment process can involve abrupt discontinuities in service levels and environmental demands.[5] Moreover, inmates find eccentric peers unsettling, and prison staff often must respond to their disruptive behavior with punitive sanctions that can exacerbate stress levels, when maladaptation is already a product—or partially a product—of serious coping deficits.[6]

Among disturbed offenders who are sent to prison, we encounter a variety of problems, but no corresponding variety of responsive dispositions. Examples of career vignettes illustrate this fact and may help students of the problem understand the dilemma that the system and its clients face in dealing with concrete and specific instances:

> An offender has broken into his neighbor's house. The police discover that he has stolen a plate of chicken wings, a bottle of wine, and a yellow garbage can. The man is hospitalized because he is "grossly psychotic" and is diagnosed as suffering from paranoid schizophrenia. He is released from the hospital, found competent, and sentenced to prison.
>
> The man commits a burglary, is surprised in the act but does not flee, though he can do so. He is declared incompetent and hospitalized. He is subsequently released with the diagnosis "brief reactive psychosis in remission, adjustment disorder with emotional features, borderline intellectual functioning, possible mild organic brain syndrome, mixed personality disorder with histrionic and borderline features, history of head trauma," and is sent to prison.
>
> The offender (who has spent most of his life in institutions) snatches the purse of a woman in a subway station. He is hospitalized for two years after his arrest, and diagnosed as suffering from schizophrenia, undifferentiated type, chronic. He is finally found competent to be tried, pleads guilty to attempted robbery, and is sentenced to prison. In the prison reception center, staff observe that the man "became increasingly withdrawn . . . sat sideways in a chair and barely

5. See H. Toch, "The disturbed disruptive inmate: Where does the bus stop? *Journal of Psychiatry and Law,* Fall 1982, 327–49.

6. For a study that shows that emotionally disturbed prisoners have relatively high rates of prison infractions, see H. Toch and K. Adams, "Pathology and disruptiveness among prison inmates," *Journal of Research in Crime and Delinquency,* 1986, *23,* 7–21.

talked." Later, they record that "continued deterioration required transfer to [the hospital]."

Some cases do involve more serious offenses which pose at least the potential for violence at the time they take place. These offenses nonetheless raise the issue of the appropriateness of prison because the offender's motives on the face of it appear to be clear products of his pathology:

> The offender, a mentally disturbed alcoholic, has no history of violence, but throws a bottle at a parked police car which injures a police officer. He cannot account for his offense. While awaiting trial, the man spends three months in hospitals, where he is maintained on thorozine. Prison staff find him "lethargic, monosyllabic . . . preoccupied" and refer him for mental health assistance.

> The offender has been a resident of several hospitals. He has been diagnosed as suffering from paranoid schizophrenia and as having drug and alcohol problems. He also has shown a propensity to carry weapons. The offense for which he is imprisoned is one in which the police find him sitting on a curb stuffing a machete down a sewer. The man has a bag with drugs, ammunition, and a handgun, and warns the police, "Don't you put any bullets in the gun." Despite the man's strange obsession, he is found competent and convicted, though diagnosed as "probable mixed personality disorder with schizotype features."

> The offender walks into a store in which his nephew works, carrying two knives and demanding money. In disarming him, the nephew is wounded. The offender is angry at his nephew, who has complained to the police because his uncle has become convinced that his family is trying to poison him. Unsurprisingly the man is diagnosed as suffering from paranoid schizophrenia and is hospitalized for nine months before he is declared competent and convicted. The man arrives in prison, "barely functional but taking his medication," and has to be transferred to the hospital.

The issue that is raised by such cases is not whether prison sentences can be legally justified. The offenders can be legitimately convicted and punished, since their culpability is usually not at issue[7] and they have been found competent. The question,

7. We have already noted that the insanity defense does not come into play for the types of offenses with which we are concerned, since the defense is in practice

rather, relates to the nature of constraints that impel judges to consider imprisonment as an option, though the record suggests that the offender who is being sentenced has obvious mental health problems. In this connection, it is necessary to admit that (1) the dispositional options that are available to the judge may be limited and often (as with offenders who are subject to mandatory sentencing provisions) are nonexistent, and (2) community-based alternatives may be sparse, because agencies can try to select their clients subject to restrictive definitions of eligibility.

Such considerations, however, do not account for the routine use of prison sentences for inmates who are disturbed, which suggests that sentencing rationales or other affirmative considerations must be at work. Closer scrutiny reveals at least two reasons that may inspire judges to consider prison as the milieu of choice for some disturbed persons.

The Prison as Backup Structure

Prison sentences are sometimes invoked for persons whose distinguishing attribute is their demonstrated incapacity to negotiate life. This observation raises the possibility that prisons may be selected on humanitarian grounds because they furnish sustenance, shelter, and supervision.[8] The third attribute (supervi-

---

invoked only when the serious offender faces heavy penalties. Seymour Halleck writes that "in our current political climate, pressure is actually growing to avoid examining psychological issues related to culpability by narrowing the insanity defense or doing away with practices associated with the diminished capacity doctrine. . . . By providing a loophole for dealing with the worst possible cases, the insanity defense allows society to acknowledge that at least some offenders are different. This enables society to avoid the formidable problems that would arise if it were to adopt a more flexible approach in assessing the relationship of psychological disability to liability in the case of all offenders" (Halleck, *The Mentally Disordered Offender*, 61).

8. The same issue arises for the parole board when it comes to releasing multiply disadvantaged offenders from prison. William McMahon, chairman of the New York State Commission of Correction, testified, for example, that developmentally disabled inmates are "less likely to receive parole, and are more likely to serve longer [prison] terms." He points out that "they are perceived as poor candidates, largely because the combination of community-based services considered essential for the success of these individuals are not available in most

sion) may be particularly prized because it ensures the availability of supportive assistance around the clock. This fact may become a prime consideration when the person who is being sentenced looks particularly helpless or lost:

> The offender has held up a gas station, has "a blank stare on his face," and is incoherent. He is found incompetent to stand trial, and he shuttles between jail and hospital for three years before he is convicted. He has been raped by fellow inmates, both in the jail and the hospital. While interviewed in the prison "he felt there was an umbrella with falling rain over his head." The interviewer's impression is that "schizophrenia is draining all of [the man's] energy" and concludes that he "needs protection or state hospitalization."
>
> The offender mugs a used car salesman and is arrested. The victim describes him as a bum "who was not all there." (The offender's history is that of a chronic hospital patient, who otherwise "leads a nomadic existence.") The man is twice declared incompetent to stand trial. After years of hospitalization he is convicted and sent to prison, where he must be committed. Prison staff point out that the man "doesn't know why he is in prison . . . lies in his cell a lot. Finds it hard to get up or get started. . . . Impresses as a man who is content with his psychological condition and has no interest in . . . participating actively in life."

The use of prisons as a supervised, multiservice environment may become attractive where less structured interventions seem to have failed to engage the offender, who appears to require more supervision, guidance, or support:

> The offender has attempted to commit a burglary. He has been resentenced as a probation violator because he is not employed and refuses to submit to vocational training. After he arrives in prison, he is referred to mental health classification "due to depression with suicidal ideation."
>
> The probation officer describes the offender as "a young man whose emotional problems have played a role in preventing him from

---

localities. Thus, the parole board believes that it is protecting the inmate and the community" (W. G. McMahon, "Testimony, New York State Assembly Standing Committee on Correction; New York State Assembly Standing Committee on Mental Health, Mental Retardation, and Developmental Disabilities, December 9, 1987").

complying with the terms and conditions of probation. . . . Curiously, he cooperated with his obligations such that he never missed a probation appointment and basically kept most of his mental health appointments as well. . . . This officer tried repeatedly to discover the source of the defendant's inhibition to look for work or accept vocational training. I can only conclude that the defendant lacks the motivation but also seems to have a genuine fear of academic/training situations which may be difficult for him to overcome. . . . He was told that probation did not exist to allow him to remain at home and do nothing with his life. The crux of the matter is that the defendant has been unwilling or unable to accept this basic premise of probation supervision."

The offender has been diagnosed as suffering from schizophrenia, chronic, undifferentiated, with mental retardation (his IQ is 67). His offense consists of a "tug of war" in which he tries to separate a lady from her handbag but fails. The offender has been paroled from prison (where he has spent most of his time hospitalized) to a civil hospital, from which he absconds. He is consequently resentenced to prison, where intake analysts point out that he "has a history of being unable to function in the community" and "has requested that the police arrest him simply so he will have somewhere to be cared for." At prison intake the man refuses to take medication, requiring an emergency commitment (the man is "eager" to be transferred to the forensic hospital) with the recommendation that "long-term psychiatric residence be provided for him in the facility and upon discharge to the community."

A more direct incentive to imprisoning the offender may exist when he has evaded or rejected community services, whose staff cannot enforce their prescriptions. The prison serves as an inviting backup, particularly where backsliding by the offender makes him a nuisance or raises the presumption (admittedly remote) that he may reoffend. In such instances the prison is seen not only as having the virtue of being escape-proof but also as serving to interdict trouble the offender seems headed for if left at large:

The man has grown up in foster homes and has graduated to psychiatric settings. He is arrested for a burglary and placed on probation. Within three months he is violated for absconding from a halfway house and not responding to treatment: He has been dismissed from an alcohol program for showing up drunk and not attending group therapy sessions.

As a child, the offender has been taken to a mental health clinic for punching a teacher in the mouth. He is convicted of stealing a motorcycle. He has done so after running away from his seventh foster home placement. He is put on probation and referred to a youth corrections program, from which he also absconds. He is placed in a residential substance abuse program, from which he again absconds, and is sentenced to prison.

Six years ago the man has committed a violent sex offense and is declared not guilty by reason of insanity. He has been committed to a hospital, from which he is released subject to conditions that include therapeutic involvements. The man's probation is revoked because he "is said to have not taken his medication on several occasions, to have missed two-thirds of his rehabilitation classes and about one-third of his therapy appointments." Prison officials find the man "distant, removed, unkempt" and "not always in touch with reality." They commit him to the forensic hospital.

The man arrives in prison ten years after he has committed his offense. The offense is an assault. The man has been involved in a family fight and ordered [by the police] to sleep in a hallway. He knifes a neighbor who objects to his presence, is placed on probation, but is later hospitalized. He is imprisoned after he rejects the hospital's discharge plan, indicating he would prefer living in men's shelters. He arrives in prison actively psychotic and is transferred to the forensic hospital.

Prison as a Secure Hospital

Some disturbed persons evoke worry about risks that relate to their self-care, including posing a danger to self; others spark concerns about the milieus in which they must function, which they can disrupt with noisy, unseemly, or destructive behavior. Such concerns are particularly inspired by offenders whose symptoms include a history of acting out, both in institutions and the community:

The offender is a patient who is given to episodes of bizarre explosive outbursts. He has been hospitalized for behavior such as running through the street nude proclaiming that he is Jesus Christ. He has also been arrested for unprovoked assaults. Jail staff note that "he goes nuts and throws things, sets fires and talks constantly. . . . He said he was a voodoo doctor and stood naked in his cell."

The offense for which the man is convicted is one in which he wakes up residents of a house, shouting at their windows that he needs money for drugs. The victims instruct the man to come to their front door, where the police arrest him. After the man arrives in prison, prison staff complain that he is "hostile, verbally aggressive, and emotionally unstable."

The man has been convicted for an incident that took place two years previously in which he set his apartment on fire. He spends much of the intervening time in a hospital, from which he is gratefully discharged with the diagnosis schizophrenia, chronic, in remission. As soon as he enters prison, the man proves disruptive, "disturbing the entire block and staff." He cannot be processed because he "shouted throughout the [intake] interview" and refused to take medication. He must be transferred to the hospital.

The offender commits a mugging during which he "made stabbing motions to the shoulder of a female victim." The victim describes the offender as "somewhat off." The man has a history of assaulting his mother, which has invited multiple hospital commitments. The diagnosis assigned him is schizophrenia, paranoid type, chronic, with acute exacerbation. In the hospital he engages in disruptive behavior, such as burning holes in sheets and setting his mattress on fire.

After the man arrives in the prison, staff write that "his adjustment is marked by continuous hallucinations with which he dialogues while in his cell, and extreme mood swings." The man sings, sometimes loudly, in his cell. Staff write [half facetiously] that "a significant feature of a positive nature is that he has a beautiful singing voice which impresses all who hear him."

The notion that prisons may be envisioned as secure hospitals, or hospital-equivalents, is in the abstract implausible. If one does not consider this possibility, however, it becomes hard to explain why hospital offenses with clear psychotic overtones result in imprisonment instead of in the upgrading of security arrangements within the hospital. The same point holds for disturbed persons who prove troublesome in community settings but are imprisoned rather than institutionalized in more treatment-relevant settings:

The man is convicted of a robbery after he is declared incompetent on five occasions, but later found competent. He serves six years, mostly in prison hospital settings.

After leaving prison, the man is sent to a civil hospital for a fifteen-day evaluation. He becomes disgruntled when his release is delayed and assaults a fellow patient who "said the wrong thing at the wrong time." He explains that "something snapped." The man is sent back to prison, where staff conclude that "he will need ongoing psychiatric care."

The offender is a badly retarded young man who sets his bed on fire because he is "angry at his brother." He is charged with committing arson but is hospitalized. While he is in the hospital, the man fondles a female fellow-patient and is again arrested. He is found fit to proceed and convicted of his sex offense.

The offender is a retarded schizophrenic. He has a long history of hospitalizations and brushes with the law. He has attempted suicide by choking himself and jumping out of a second-story window. In the hospital he enters the rooms of other patients looking for money, takes a wallet, and is caught. He is declared incompetent but is later sent to prison on a guilty plea for attempted burglary. The prison finds that "obviously, he is a disturbed psychiatric patient" and commits him to the forensic hospital. Staff note that "he prefers the role of patient and is a difficult client whose prognosis is bleak."

The offender is a mentally retarded man who has been convicted of rape after engaging in intercourse with a fourteen-year-old agency client who "apparently [was] a willing participant." The man has sustained brain damage as the result of an accident in which he was involved as a child. He has subsequently experienced "nervous breakdowns," has attempted suicide, and been diagnosed as suffering from a schizoid personality disorder.

A final category of imprisoned offenders enhances the plausibility of the "secure hospital" image of the prison, because the offenders at issue are persons who are imprisoned after becoming destructively refractory in other settings. These offenders are not only difficult to manage, but also react violently to efforts to manage them. The other side of the coin is that these persons are not premeditatedly violent but are clearly disturbed at the time they pose a danger to their treaters. The relevancy of this second fact to sentencing authorities recedes, however, given the safety concerns of treatment staff, which seem to underlie community demands for prison sentences:

The offender is a severely retarded man who has become convinced that staff of a mental health program are laughing at him. He sets fire to the agency's building and tries to burn down its van. He throws bottles at agency staff and arrives there with a knife in his pocket announcing he intends to stab someone. He also threatens to rape a social worker attached to the agency.

The man is sent to jail, where he is repeatedly raped. He is declared competent, pleads guilty to Arson 2, and is sent to prison with a long sentence.

The man is a former hospital patient who is imprisoned for arson after he sets fire to a group therapy room in an outpatient clinic where he is treated. While he is being arrested the man is described as "rambling continuously." He makes statements such as "it was a political arrest," "there is a question of constitutionality involved here; I didn't want to gain any more weight," "it was all after the fact, and there is defamation involved," "I got lonely and I wanted to be with my people at the clinic," and "I never got over the first hump." The man is subjected to competency examinations, but is declared competent, convicted, and imprisoned. In the prison, according to staff, he "suddenly experienced a full psychotic breakdown."

The offender has been sentenced to probation for assaulting his girlfriend. At the time he is diagnosed as experiencing a "depressive reaction with paranoid features." Six years later the man has a psychotic breakdown after he is fired from his job and evicted from his room for "bizarre" behavior. While disturbed he enters his probation office and refuses to leave. He ransacks the office, traps the staff behind desks, and threatens to assault them. He is restrained and removed from the premises. His probation is revoked, and he is resentenced to prison, where he arrives medicated, and is adjudged "friendly and cooperative."

The man has a long career as a hospital patient. His offense takes place in the hospital in which he is confined. There he assaults a psychiatrist, breaking a chair over his head. He also destroys windows at the nurses' station before he is subdued. In the past, he has assaulted a social worker and tried to choke an attendant. In jail the man attacks a corrections supervisor, who loses two teeth. In prison, he threatens to "deck" correction officers at the reception center. Staff write that he "impressed as having limited intellect, horizons and mental sophistication."

What Is to Be Done?

The illustrations we have provided document our impression that disturbed persons are sometimes adjudicated in surprisingly routine fashion as they are sentenced to imprisonment. We infer that the probability of such prison sentences is enhanced in cases in which (1) offenders have failed to respond to community programs, or (2) have proved disruptive to community settings. In neither case can the concern of sentencing authorities be adjudged misplaced, but it is also not obvious that prison is the most appropriate solution to these concerns.

The difficulty lies in the fact that the hypothetical type of setting that *does* address concerns about the need for support and structure for disturbed persons does not at present exist, and public pressures are not being exerted to create such a setting. This indifference is understandable because (1) the types of persons we have described are rejected individuals who have no constituency, (2) they do not fit neatly into service-related classifications,[9] (3) once offenders are in prison, they are invisible to the public, as are the problems they experience, and (4) prisons are institutions of last resort; they have the obligation to deal with their inmates, even if they have proven to be inhospitable and thankless clients elsewhere. The dilemma is further compounded by the fact that a problem person can become a correctional client for life on the installment plan, because once he has been in prison his chances of being recycled into prison are enhanced.

Considering the problems created for the prison by nonserious

9. Commissioner Coughlin notes, for example, that "it is abundantly clear that a person suffering from mental retardation and some form of mental illness is the bain of everyone's existence. The retardation people point to the mental illness and throw their hands up. The mental health people point to the retardation and do the same. . . . The current practice of labelling everything just reinforces this process. I once proposed a State Department of Dual Diagnosis, so that no one could hide behind a label" (Coughlin, personal communication). McMahon (see note 8) concurs. He testified that "in the case of the dual diagnosed, it is difficult to access services because (agencies) have difficulty agreeing upon primary responsibility." He cites as an added problem the fact that "residential and treatment programs, in general, avoid persons with a criminal record."

disturbed offenders and the unimpressive, checkered careers they demonstrate, must we accept their prevalance as prison inmates? Prison officials do not think so, for their agency's sake and that of their charges. Judges should probably not think so either, because the integrity of their profession is demeaned whenever they send a person to prison by default rather than because he or she belongs there.

Admittedly it is easier to delineate the current situation than it is to envisage its resolution. The best we can hope for is that the future of forensic psychiatry and psychology may come to include more serious input into sentencing and involvement in the creation of programs that can divert offenders before or after they are sentenced.[10] We can also hope for interagency arrangements and hybrid systems in the community that will willingly accommodate persons who now fall between the cracks, most notably those impaired, disabled, and disturbed men and women who inappropriately become correctional clients because we honestly do not know what else to do with them.[11]

10. In New York State, the Office of Mental Health Bureau of Forensic Services and the Division of Probation and Correctional Alternatives are in the process of shaping an "Alternatives to Incarceration" proposal which would "define and make available to the courts alternative sentencing options for cases involving mentally ill non-violent offenders." The proposal suggests refining and evaluating models in two state counties and assisting other interested counties with the development of diversion program (Joel Dvoskin, personal communication). One attribute of such programs which is critical is to enable them to cover gaps between service modalities with hybrid organizational arrangements that make it difficult to reject multiproblem clients because they do not "fit." McMahon (see note 8) made this point when he testified that "I believe that the problems of the developmentally disabled offender can most effectively be addressed by utilizing a multidisciplinary, inter-agency approach."

The most modest possible arrangement that can address the problem of sentencing involves screening suspected arrestees before they are charged. E. Hochstedler describes the work of a Mental Health Screening Unit operating out of a Wisconsin prosecutor's office ("Criminal prosecution of the mentally disordered: A descriptive analysis," *Criminal Justice Review*, 1987, *12*, 1–11). She observes that prosecutors may deliberately charge offenders as a means of imposing treatment arrangements where such persons would not be civilly committable. She also notes that "judges show leniency at the final disposition to those who receive treatment, either as a condition of pretrial release or while being examined for competency to stand trial" (10).

11. The problem is most acute for seriously retarded offenders, for whom new types of facilities may have to be envisaged. This point has been made by (among others) Beverly Rowan, in a position paper prepared for the President's Committee on Mental Retardation. Rowan writes,

> Special facilities should be created to handle mentally retarded offenders in a more intelligent, humane, and effective manner. These facilities should be more secure than state institutions for the retarded, but free from the perverse influences found in standard training schools or prisons. They should be located near institutions of higher learning so that students, professors, and qualified corrections people will be available to assist with habilitation problems. (Principal Paper, Correction Section, in M. Kindred, et al., *The Mentally Retarded Citizen and the Law* [New York: Free Press, 1976])

Chapter 9

The Extremely Disturbed and Extremely Violent Offender: The Problem of Programing

In a sense, the dictum "history is destiny" provides an empirically testable hypothesis in studying individual careers. Some persons will be found to behave in patterned, redundant fashion, and others will show the ability to change for the better (or worse). Recidivism refers to one form of predestination—not escaping from a propensity to engage in undesirable conduct.

Whether persons who have a history of emotional problems will remain "disturbed" is a crucial issue for those who deal with such persons. Where historically derived measures describe continuing patterns of maladaptation they carry substantial implications having to do with the desirability of prevention or the need for treatment.

We have followed all of our disturbed offenders into the prison to ascertain whether they still need mental health services when they arrive there. The summary results of this inquiry (table 9.1) show that only 4 percent of inmates who have not received mental health services in the community will require them in prison. This modest figure compares to 43 percent for the inmates who have mental health histories and 36 percent for inmates with "mixed" histories which include substance abuse services. Substance abuse histories alone yield a 10 percent service-delivery figure.

Table 9.1. Mental health services required during first two years of incarceration by offenders in our four samples

The offender's mental health history	Screening by staff	Outpatient services	Hospitalization Single	Multiple
No history (n = 544)	16.9%	3.7%	0.02%	0%
Substance abuse (n = 83)	18.1	9.6	0	0
Psychiatric (n = 540)	20.4	29.3	7.2	6.3
Combined substance abuse and psychiatric (n = 141)	21.3	29.8	4.3	1.4

Commitments to the prison psychiatric hospital, which presuppose very serious illness, are called for with one of seven members of the psychiatric sample, but only one of twenty inmates with "mixed" histories. One lone inmate in the comparison sample (out of the total group of 544) required hospitalization.

These results are quite surprising given that a large number of inmates in the four groups are screened, usually at intake and for the parole board. We also know that guards, who refer most inmates for service by mental health staff, have no access to mental health files.

Which are the disturbed inmates who need assistance in prison? Several clusters disproportionately account for mental health clients (table 9.2). Heading the list are the Acute Disturbed Exploders, 39 percent of whom will be hospitalized. We recall that this group has (unsurprisingly) extensive mental health involvements, particularly recently. Its violence is often eccentric (see chapter 7) and is always extreme, though the offenders have no violence histories and low arrest records. In this respect these inmates differ from Chronic Disturbed Exploders, whom they otherwise resemble. This Exploder group—which we have described as extreme violent recidivists with long-term mental health difficulties—has less serious problems in the prison, though half the group (51 percent) needs mental health services. The third most violent cluster in the sample is Disturbed Sex

Table 9.2. Mental health services required during the first two years of incarceration by offenders with mental health histories

| | Mental health service provided | | | |
	Screening by staff	Outpatient services	Hospitalization Single	Multiple
Psychiatric history offenders				
Impulsive burglar	36%	21%	5%	0%
Impulsive robber	26	18	5	0
Long-term explosive robber	25	30	0	4
Young explosive robber	38	15	0	0
Mature mugger	9	32	5	5
Acute disturbed exploder	16	25	25	14
Chronic disturbed exploder	13	42	6	3
Disturbed sex offender	17	32	9	17
Composite career offender	17	25	7	8
Compensatory offender	21	37	11	0
Combined substance abuse and psychiatric history offenders				
Dependent burglar	20%	25%	0%	0%
Skid row robber	44	22	0	0
Skid row exploder	14	31	9	3
Compounded career offender	14	32	3	0
Multi-problem robber	29	32	7	0

Offenders, 26 percent of whom are hospitalized. The group records the third highest rate of eccentric offenses and has a substantial history of mental health involvements but a limited offense history.

Our findings are dramatic and consistent: Persons who are disturbed *after* they offend tend to be disturbed *before* they offend, and when we look at the samples in more detail we discover that the most disturbed inmates have committed the most extreme violence and mostly the "craziest" violence. This trend continues upon inspection: the fourth most disturbed group (the Compensatory Career Offenders) proves to be the fourth most violent group, and the most disturbed cluster in the mixed sample (Skid Row Exploders) is responsible for the most serious violence in the sample. We conclude that there exists a clear-cut type we can call the seriously disturbed violent offender—meaning an offender who is extremely violent when he offends and is chronically disturbed. This chapter will deal with the question of what to do with such offenders.

The Insanity Defense Revisited

If the insanity defense were more frequently invoked, fewer seriously disturbed violent offenders would be in prison because they could lay claim to being adjudged insane. This is so because their mental health problems are mostly contemporary with their crimes, which at least makes it reasonable for psychiatric testimony to be invited. The offenses the group commits are also consequential, which makes an expensive defense more cost-effective.

If the offenders we describe had offended in continental Europe, many would be acquitted of their crimes because continental insanity rules are at times broader than those that fall in the McNaghten tradition.[1] These European offenders would not walk free, of course, any more than they would if they were acquitted in the United States. Insanity acquittees everywhere earn terms of hospitalization, which are less determinate than prison sentences. In practice this means that hospital terms may prove longer or shorter than prison terms, but one cannot predict whether they will be longer or shorter. Civil libertarians focus on the possibility that hospital terms can prove longer than the prison sentences offenders would otherwise serve. The average member of the public, on the other hand, worries that hospitalization may release the offender earlier, with the double result that he will be insufficiently punished and will pose danger of re-

1. In Norway an offender who is known to have been psychotic at the time of his offense is found not guilty even if there is no alleged connection between his psychosis and his offense. Other European countries use standards that approximate the Durham rule (see M. Roth and R. Bluglass, eds., *Psychiatry, Human Rights and the Law* (Cambridge, Cambridge University Press, 1985).

newed predation. The public also does not trust hospital psychiatrists (who are presumed to have offender-centered concerns) to consider the interests of crime victims.

Less controversy would occur if the insanity defense were invoked primarily for nonserious offenses (see chapter 8), since in such offenses no victims have been hurt. The absence of injuries that cry out for redress would make it easier for the courts to center on the offenders' state of mind and to consider community treatment for them. At worst, offenders could always be subjected to short-term hospitalization, with discharge criteria uninflated by public concern, revulsion, and risk considerations. Since substantial penalties would not be at issue, it might also be possible to make the dispositional process in practice less adversarial, dispensing with battles of experts and working out solutions through plea bargains.

The atrophy over time of the insanity defense in trials of serious violent offenders creates a situation that accomplishes two results: It makes the amount of time the offender serves more predictable, and reassures the public that offenders will "pay" for their crimes. On the other side of the ledger, the nonuse of insanity pleas has consequences that muddy the waters of public policy. Among these are (1) the fact that persons are convicted who do not resemble the coldblooded offenders envisaged in statutes and could hypothetically be held nonresponsible for their crimes; (2) the fact that there are only evanescent differences between many persons who get convicted and insanity acquittees, which raises the specter of discrimination based on the availability of defense funds or other unfair considerations; and (3) the point we have already discussed, that the influx of disturbed offenders makes prisons repositories of inmates for whom prisons were not ideally designed.

In the long run, to be sure, the nonuse of the insanity defense makes little difference. Disturbed offenders need mental health services no matter where they are sent, and such services must be provided by mental health staff in one setting or the other. To be sure, most mental health staff prefer to work in hospitals, but close reflection might tell them that the prison may have some advantages as a place in which to treat violence-prone persons.

Among these advantages are that prisons are unquestionably secure, which means that staff and fellow residents are protected from the violence of explosive inmates, and the escape of such inmates is unlikely. Mental health staff in the prison also need not decide when to release potential troublemakers into the community, which is a "damned if you do, damned if you don't" type of assignment. On the other hand, a mental health staff member who works in the prison is a guest of prison officials, whose concerns must be respected.[2]

Mental health staff may also find the prison discomfitting because prisons are self-consciously nonrehabilitative, though corrections has not been able to stake out a positive mission other than keeping offenders off the streets.[3] Given the obvious ambiguity of the prison's goal the mental health staff member, whose role is uncertain to begin with, has an even harder time defining a defensible mission for himself.

The authors of a recent survey of prison mental health services write that

> strong disagreement still exists in a number of areas regarding what services are proper and appropriate for prisoners who desire or are in need of mental health services. Those with a client-centered perspective operate out of a totally different philosophy from those with an institution-centered perspective. One extreme regards the mentally disordered prisoner as entitled to the care and privacy one

2. An example of mental health staff's concern with this issue is a prison standard proposed by the American Association of Correctional Psychologists, which reads, "The psychologists, and the staff activities for which these individuals are responsible, [must] have professional autonomy regarding psychological services, within the constraints of appropriate security regulations applicable to all institutional personnel, such regulations being in conformity with the written directives of institutions and or headquarters" (American Association of Correctional Psychologists, "Standards for psychological services in adult jails and prison," *Criminal Justice and Behavior*, 1980, 7, 81–127, p. 89.

3. We have mentioned elsewhere that "though nature abhors a vacuum, corrections lives with one in disquietingly unnatural comfort. The rejection of rehabilitative goals has created a reluctance to define a new mission. The closest approximation we have makes prisons the handmaidens of dispassionately vengeful courts" (H. Toch, "Quo vadis?" *Canadian Journal of Criminology*, 1984, 26, 511–16, p. 511.

would enjoy in the private and civilian sector; the other, focused on maintaining order and discipline in a large correctional setting, desires as little differentiation as possible in the administration of rules and sanctions. If we add to this the bureaucratic infighting endemic within and between agencies, it is hardly surprising that no one has come to total agreement on the subject. Without consensus on policy, however, and without the dollars to back up the policy, major conflicts break out among the personnel actually charged with prisoner management, and the disparity between service levels at different institutions grows.[4]

The Disturbed Offender in Hospitals

The problems associated with mental health services in prisons may be serious, but one must recognize that mental hospitals have counterpart problems in dealing with serious violent offenders.

Mental hospitals, like prisons, are in a continuing state of transition. The transitions of prisons and hospitals, however, are opposite, or at least disparate. Prisons are expanding their purview and are holding convicts for longer periods of time. Hospitals are shrinking their clientele and are releasing patients as quickly as they can, continuing to treat them (or referring them for treatment) on an outpatient basis. Today's hospital population is usually more seriously disturbed, and the hospital's aim is to "stabilize" the condition of patients so it can be dealt with—in theory at least—in the community.

The disturbed offender fits uncomfortably into the contemporary hospital's mission. For one, the serious offender cannot be quickly stabilized and released under medication because the community will not tolerate the risk this entails. As a consequence the disturbed offender has to remain on hospital wards for long periods of time, until he is certified as nondangerous as well as nondisturbed. In the past, this would have been par for the psychiatric course, but today it means that the offender may be

4. K. H. Gohlke, "Executive summary," in National Institute of Corrections, *Source Book on the Mentally Disordered Prisoner* (Washington, D.C.: Department of Justice, 1985), 3.

surrounded by persons who are more disturbed than himself, while in the prison the offender's peers would be nondisturbed offenders serving sentences as long as (or longer than) his own. In the hospital the offender also carries the stigma of his offense. Mental health staff who work in hospitals are apt to be intimidated by violence and may approach the offender uneasily and with fear.[5] This creates problems for staff morale, but it can also affect patient care because staff apprehension leads to overmedication as a reassuring "management" tool.[6]

5. J. R. Lion and S. A. Pasternak, "Countertransference reactions to violent patients," *American Journal of Psychiatry,* 1973, *130,* 207–10. The fears of mental health staff may sometimes be reinforced by the advice that these staff receive from correctional experts. A sample injunction is the following:

> The psychiatrist should be keenly aware of his own safety. When unfamiliar with an inmate who has been recently violent, he should inquire into his present behavior before seeing him. If there is any uncertainty regarding the inmate's present state of control, he should not hesitate to interview the inmate in the doorway of his cell with an officer at arm's length. (U.S. Bureau of Prisons: *A Handbook of Correctional Psychiatry,* vol. 1 (Washington, D.C.: Department of Justice, 1968), 20)

The same source also tells its readers that

> failure to face his fear and hostility will lead the psychiatrist to reject the violent inmate and withdraw from the focal activity of the prison. Facing these fears partially can lead to an over-identification with the inmate and diatribes against "inhumane" treatment. Facing his fears fully, however, will allow him to help the inmate and the staff. (Ibid., 21)

6. The author of a survey of mental health services points out that "many prison medical staff members admit that medication is used as much for custody purposes as for medical purposes" (R. Wilson, "Who will care for the 'mad and bad'?" *Corrections Magazine,* February 1980, p. 10). A similar impression prevails in other settings in which psychotropic medication is used. An authority on medication in civil hospitals, for example, records,

> This author has often seen the "snow phenomenon" whereby a patient is viewed as exceedingly dangerous and assaultive, given large amounts of medication, and secluded and put in what is tantamount to sensory deprivation. Fearful of being in a locked room, the patient's behavior escalates and becomes loud and boisterous. Nursing staff become more frightened and ask the doctor to prescribe more medication. The medication is administered parenterally without any verbal discussion, the patient's condition worsens leading to more medication, and a vicious cycle ensues. This situation can be reversed both by

Medication is a key issue in hospitals because psychotropic drugs are the therapeutic modality of choice in most psychiatric settings. This is not in itself a problem but becomes a problem if we envisage treatment goals for the offender other than reducing or deleting the symptoms of his psychosis. If we have a subsidiary concern with contributing to offender socialization, the hospital has some advantages over the prison—it can be more democratic, for instance—but it has particularly serious disadvantages, such as the fact that one cannot rehearse prosocial living where the prevailing concern is with humane storage pending the elimination of florid symptomatology.

The Disturbed Offender in Prison

The other side of the coin we are viewing is that prisons are not designed to accommodate psychotics, who are apt to behave in eccentric ways. Two features of prison pose particular problems for the disturbed inmate. The first is that prisons insist on at least a minimal amount of participation in prison routines, which include self-care, following instructions, and involvement in programs. Opting out of prison life results in a cumulation of write-ups or disciplinary infractions, which invite punishment no matter how "crazily" motivated the inmate's lapses may be.[7]

---

taking the patient out of seclusion and lowering his medication. (J. R. Lion, "Special aspects of psychopharmacology," in J. R. Lion and W. H. Reid, *Assaults within Psychiatric Facilities* [New York: Grune and Stratton, 1963], 290)

The same authority mentions that medication can lead to the exacerbation of mental health problems, including depression and suicide:

> Violence in an aggressive patient can be controlled through complete sedation, but that is not an acceptable goal. The goal of drug treatment should be to curb the impulsivity and lability of the patient so that he or she thinks before acting and speaks while thinking, thus allowing for conflict resolution. This is a delicate task. The author has seen a profound depression develop in patients whose aggression was "quenched by drugs," and who were then, for interesting and complex reasons, unable to vent their anger but were forced to channel it inwardly. (Ibid., 294)

7. H. Toch and K. Adams, with J. D. Grant, *Coping: Maladaptation in the Prison* (New Brunswick, N.J.: Transaction, 1989).

A second feature of prison is that it requires close cohabitation among persons who must depend on each other not to increase discomforts built into the prison experience or to pose risks of harm to their peers. Eccentricity—especially unpredictable eccentricity—creates discomfort for prison staff and inmates because it makes the environment less dependable. Disturbed offenders also invite predation from fellow inmates when they appear vulnerable, or pose risks to inmates and staff when they unpredictably explode.[8]

Another problem is one of logistics. Disturbed persons are invariably unstable and require gradations of mental health assistance, ranging from hospitalization to "normalcy." If one is serious about responding to changing needs of clients in any routinized setting this means that one must shuttle them from place to place, so as to adjust their regime and social milieu to accommodate the changes in their condition. This becomes a particularly serious issue when a person needs hospitalization. Hospital commitments must usually be approved by the courts and require shifting jurisdiction from corrections to mental health staff. Among the typical squabbles this invites is that hospitals may regard some of the inmates referred to them as insufficiently disturbed, and prisons may view the inmates as insufficiently recovered when they return.[9]

Many prison systems have an insufficient range of options to accommodate offenders whose condition falls short of meeting hospital commitment criteria. And later, when the inmate is moved from the hospital to a different setting, the sharp transition can undo whatever benefit hospitalization offers because stabilization (the standard goal of inpatient treatment) presup-

8. Ibid.; also see Toch, *Men in Crisis*.

9. Wilson writes that "a common criticism by psychiatrists of prison administrators is that they want the doctors to handle the problem cases, which are not always psychiatric problems" ("Who will care for the 'mad' and 'bad'?" 14). The other side of the coin is that mental health staff may classify a disturbed offender as "not a psychiatric problem" if he appears overly threatening. Wilson quotes an official of the American Medical Association, for example, who admits that "the mental health administrators don't want to monkey around with acting-out clients, so they send them back" (8).

poses aftercare, including outpatient services.[10] In the community the unavailability of lower-order mental health assistance contributes to homelessness and to vagrancy patterns that include involvement in crime.[11] In the prison, unrecovered patients often become disciplinary problems, and this creates a vicious cycle if punishment exacerbates the mental health problems of some of the inmates.

Above all, prisons must determine to what extent they are in the business of providing mental health assistance. Such a determination, however, is not simple because the line between rehabilitation and mental health services is hard to draw. The courts have determined that inmates have a "right to treatment" to

10. Commuting between hospital and prison settings is referred to as "bus therapy," especially by observers who see the practice as detrimental. Freeman, Dinitz, and Conrad, for example, write that "until courts can establish rules to govern the disposition of such inmates their programming will be punctuated by bus movements which are clearly not intended for their benefit" (R. A. Freeman, S. Dinitz, and J. P. Conrad, "A look at the dangerous offender and society's effort to control him," *American Journal of Correction*, January–February 1977, 25–31, p. 30.

11. A recent *Newsweek* review concluded that an estimated 1.5 million mentally ill persons now live in the community. *Newsweek* points out that

> In truth, virtually any of those 1.5 million patients can be "homeless" at one time or another, for a chronic disease like schizophrenia tends to be cyclical, and its victims usually veer from periods of fragile stability to intermittent breakdowns all their lives. . . . What is missing from their lives is effective community care—and without exception, mental-health professionals say the nation has reneged on that promise . . . the norm in most state or local agencies is a level of care so minimal as to approach official negligence—and in city after city, despairing mental-health workers concede that the system as a whole fails abysmally ("Clearing the hospitals," *Newsweek*, January 21, 1986)

Newsweek's impression is confirmed by most mental health personnel who work with homeless persons. A psychiatrist who has made the rounds of downtown New York City, for example, observes,

> There were disabilities more florid than I had seen before; people lost in the utter apathy that schizophrenia can breed and others fighting through a paranoid world of delusional villains out to ensnare them. These disorders are found in abundance in mental hospitals, but there medications blunt their full force. On Broadway the diseased mind is free to torment its victim relentlessly (D. Goleman, "To expert eyes, city streets are open mental wards," *New York Times*, November 4, 1986, p. C1).

preserve health, but it is not clear how much "mental health" is included in the "health" which must be preserved in the prison. The legal formula implies that the goal of the therapy one must provide to inmates is to help them reduce symptoms that disable them and make them suffer.[12] But substandard mental health is a continuum of symptoms or suffering, and lines can be more or less generously drawn. Another problem is that there is an unascertainable connection between the offenses of inmates and their psychological handicaps, which obfuscates the line between correctional goals and treatment. More relevantly, emotional problems can affect prison adjustment, which is a concern of prison administrators. Even if a mental health staff member did not wish to assist his or her warden to preserve security it is hard to envision successful therapy that would not improve prison behavior, since the inmate's difficulties can be observed (and addressed) only in encounters that arise in the prison. If the inmate becomes better adjusted, he should therefore become a better inmate.

Putting aside issues of mental health goals, we can turn to consider what some of the choices are for corrections if it wishes to create a program that meets the needs of the disturbed violent inmate, those of the prison, and those of society to which the inmate must return.

12. In discussing the rights of disturbed prison inmates, F. Cohen points out,

For example, a constitutional right to treatment might be fashioned as a right to the most thorough diagnosis and the most skillful treatment available for the particular condition. A mentally retarded inmate might be entitled to such habilitative efforts as will maximize his human potential. On the other hand, such rights could be constructed to require only that some medical or professional judgment be brought to bear to identify and then to provide minimally acceptable care in order to avoid death or needless suffering.

As the text will make clear, the constitutional right to treatment is much closer to the second construction than the first. The most important point we must make here is that constitutional minima in this (or any other) area must not be confused with desirable governmental policy, desirable professional practices or standards, or desirable penal practices or standards. (F. Cohen, "Legal issues and the mentally disordered offender," in National Institute of Corrections, *Sourcebook on the Mentally Disordered Prisoner*, [Washington, D.C.: Department of Justice, 1985], 33)

A Program for Disturbed Violent Offenders

Any program for disturbed violent offenders must recognize that this group of offenders will contain persons with chronic mental health problems. However, this does not mean that all offenders in high-risk groups have chronic problems or that chronic problems are problems that remain at the same level of seriousness all the time. The approach to the offender must, therefore, be open-ended, invoking mental health assistance as it is needed and when it is needed. Beyond this requisite there are some questions that any program designer must resolve, and the answers to these are less clear-cut.

Homogeneity of the Population

There are advantages in working with a group of offenders who have similar problems, such as the members of any of our clusters. These advantages increase if one's task includes rehabilitative concerns, because homogeneity means that offenses are similar in kind. Other problems one may wish to address can also become more comparable if one's clients have reached a commensurate stage of life and if they share similarities of background. The most noteworthy advantages accrue if one envisages a therapeutic community in which peer interactions are important and the compatibility of inmates matters.[13]

Homogeneity, however, reduces size, and where prisons are crowded few systems can afford small, specialized programs. A compromise structure involves combining clusters, which can be subdivided for certain purposes (such as treatment) and recombined for others. One advantage of this model is that an offender may be assigned to a group concerned with violence (in which Disturbed Sex Offender A may be paired with Disturbed Sex Offenders B, C, and D because they share the same offense background) and to a different group concerned with mental health–related issues (in which Offender A might be paired with Offenders E, F, and G, who are schizophrenics in remission or

13. H. Toch, ed., *Therapeutic Communities in Corrections* (New York: Praeger, 1980).

have become chronic disciplinary violators). More heterogeneous groups can also be formed around issues of living in a prison unit or for helping staff run a program or around activities such as academic self-study.

Segregation of the Program Population

The inmates we have described often cause problems, and have problems, in the prison. The fact that the inmates are at times troublesome or disturbed argues for a separate setting—even a separate facility—which can be part of the system and at the same time have a measure of autonomy. One advantage of autonomy is that it introduces flexibility, if one wants or needs it. Some prison routines—such as the operation of the disciplinary process—could thus be relaxed if necessary.[14] More important, in a special setting one can afford tolerance of deviance, which is difficult in the prison. A special setting, however, must not be too special. If one assigns an inmate to a program known as containing eccentric or dangerous individuals one risks stigmatizing him or creating a ghetto from which it is difficult to escape.

Ingress and Egress in a Program

The problem of ghetto existence can be partly addressed by regarding program participation as time-bound and as a phase of the inmate's career defined by his progress. An offender can

14. The administrators of an interdisciplinary program for disturbed offenders in Pennsylvania provide a case in point. They write,

> At one point the Bureau of Corrections wished to implement a procedure whereby hospital staff would be required to formally report any infraction of the rules to the prison for inclusion on the patient's record. Treatment staff felt this procedure would be countertherapeutic in that such infractions, which are often a product of the patient's illness, if reported, would interfere with treatment processes aimed at eventual release via parole. An agreement was eventually reached whereby minor infractions would continue to be handled by the unit disciplinary committee and not entered on the record, while major infractions (serious fights, escapes, etc.) would require formal reporting to Corrections. (M. K. Cooke and G. Cooke, "An integrated program for mentally ill offenders: Description and evaluation," *International Journal of Offender Therapy and Comparative Criminology,* 1982, *26,* 53–61, pp. 53–54)

become a program resident at prison intake or later if staff feel that he can benefit from special placement. The presumption would be that the inmate can graduate from the program or be transferred to some other program when he is ready to make the transition.[15]

The virtue of this approach is that it expects and accommodates change. It permits "mainstreaming" of inmates whose problems dissipate over time but allows for formal mental health assistance, or more specialized services, for inmates who cannot adjust to a midrange program.

Staff Teaming

Programs for inmates who are disturbed require involvement of mental health staff. Such staff may be invoked for individual inmates as needed, but this arrangement invites jurisdictional problems between types of staff and compartmentalizes services. A more integrated solution is to use teams which include mental health workers and correctional officers.[16] Staff of both kinds benefit from such teaming because it offers cross-fertilization and democratization of roles. The inmate also benefits because the stigma of labeling him as sick is reduced. Where all staff deal with all inmates no lines need be drawn (or emphasized) that differentiate "disturbed" and "nondisturbed" inmates, which is in any event an artificial distinction.

15. Fairweather and his colleagues emphasize that this requisite is essential to any mental health programs that play a transitional role between the hospital and the streets (G. W. Fairweather, D. H. Sanders, D. L. Cressler, and H. Maynard, *Community Life for the Mentally Ill,* [Chicago: Aldine, 1969]).

16. The Pennsylvania program referred to in note 14 above describes its staffing as follows:

[The program] was administered jointly by the Bureau of Corrections and the Department of Welfare. Correctional personnel included an on-site full-time project coordinator, as well as the security staff (correctional officers). Hospital personnel included psychiatric aides, nurses, psychiatrists, psychologists, social workers and auxiliary treatment personnel. Hospital and correctional personnel jointly comprised the treatment team. (Cooke and Cooke, "An integrated program," 53. Also see Toch, *Therapeutic Communities*)

Building in a Research Component

We began by noting that disturbed violent offenders are a badly unexplored entity, and we admit that we have far from exhausted the topic as a subject of research. The concentrated availability of a study population of such offenders provides an opportunity to add to our knowledge about this important subject. An officially designated research mission can enhance the role of a prison program because staff can see themselves serving a larger cause than the program itself. This sort of mission also underlines the importance of keeping records, such as of interview summaries (or transcripts) and the minutes of group meetings.[17] A research function can appeal even to inmates, who can rationalize that they are providing data (with appropriate assurance of confidentiality) when they share intimate problems and concerns.

Providing Treatment

We have not said much about our program's treatment goals, but we can delineate some options. These options include attending to mental health problems and reducing violence recidivism (which entails studying violence), but one can also try to reach some more general goal—such as enhancing living skills—which encompasses the other objectives.

---

17. Such information can prove useful in extending our knowledge about the causal connections between emotional problems and violent acts. One author concerned with such links, for example, concludes that

> extensive accounts—both spontaneous and structured—from the subject and as many other sources as possible of a violent act, the mental state around the time of that act and states of both pre-act health and social adjustment are thus all important. Collection and integration of many such accounts, and comparison of these between schizophrenic and non-psychotic groups will clarify ways in which the illness has been important and, I believe, identify subgroups who are particularly violence prone, perhaps improving our predictions about the risks of violence. Only then can the role of psychiatrists and of available treatments in managing the violence, even of a psychotic group, be clarified. (P. Taylor, "Schizophrenia and violence," in J. Gunn and D. P. Farrington, *Abnormal Offenders, Delinquency and the Criminal Justice System* [London: Wiley, 1982], 281)

Recidivism reduction is no doubt the riskiest goal one can claim, and the hardest to defend. For one, some would argue that mental health problems are not the most plausible selection criterion for inmates if recidivism is one's concern. Monahan and Steadman, for example, write,

> If the effectiveness of therapeutic techniques is to be measured against the criterion of reduced criminal recidivism, those techniques should be targeted directly against recidivism, not against mental disorder as an intervening variable. There may, for example, be a small group of "psychotic rapists" for whom the cure of their psychosis will result in the cessation of their raping. But there may also be a much larger group of nonpsychotic rapists—or rapists for whom psychosis and criminal tendencies coexist without being causally related—for whom psychological techniques aimed directly at reducing recidivism (e.g. training in self-control and socially appropriate forms of making sexual requests) would prove effective. The use of such techniques, of course, would leave any existing mental disorder intact.[18]

One problem we see with this view of goals is that it implies that offenders can be subdivided into compartments, some of which may be watertight, so that they can be filled or emptied without affecting each other. In practice, rehabilitators try to change people for the better and hope for outcomes on as many fronts as possible.

The example offered in the quote is also misleading, because the criterion it proposes for the pairing of targets is their offense alone. If we pool disturbed and nondisturbed rapists the assumption is that rapists are more similar to each other than are rapists and similarly motivated offenders (such as arsonists) who have comparable backgrounds and dispositions. We also imply with such pairing that we can address the behavior (rape) without worrying about why it occurs. This presumption would in fact be particularly surprising with rape, which ranges from subcultural gang activity to sadistic, pathologically tinged rage.

On the other hand it would be shortsighted to work with offenders without considering the offenses they have committed.

---

18. Monahan and Steadman, "Crime and mental disorder," 183.

Many crimes express broader behavior trends which we can hope to observe in nonoffense settings. This holds particularly true of violence, which reflects dispositions such as suspiciousness, explosiveness, egocentricity, and limited acumen. When one takes a closer look at violent offenses (as we have done in examples) thematic content can be seen which simultaneously emerges— usually in attenuated form—in everyday behavior.

Continuity of motive also operates in the other direction, and we have a right to assume that improvements we can effect (enhanced competence, mental health, or interpersonal skill) may modulate some offense behavior. This does not justify defending treatment as a way to reduce recidivism, but we can hope that there may be crime-related outcomes to tangible behavioral improvement, which we can document with behavior we can observe. The behavior we must attend to will of course vary with the person and his level of pathology. It can range from taking showers to respectful demeanor with authority figures to not losing one's cool, being predatory, and posturing toughness in compensatory ways.

Treatment goals that address observable deficits are not mental health restoration or rehabilitation but can approximate such objectives, depending on the transfer that occurs. The intervening goal we must have in mind in working with disturbed violent persons must be to incrementally improve mental health and/or reduce violence potential.

The gains in most instances will be modest. The fact that they can also on occasion be dramatic need not unduly excite us. Such results must be placed in the same hopper as the fact that on other occasions program graduates will revert to mental illness, or to crime. Neither development can be unambiguously ascribed to change agents whose jurisdiction ends once the offender is released.

Recidivism would be saliently at issue if aftercare extended into the community, which would be possible if halfway settings were available under parole auspices. We have noted that coping abilities in life cannot be challenged in institutions because the range of challenges institutional settings offer—even of painful challenges—is narrow. What institutions can provide is a combination of constraint and support (staff call it structure) which reduces temptations and helps vulnerable persons to survive. Persons without support who need support use sudden freedom to flounder and fail. Freed psychotics develop anxiety when they meet complexity. Absent constraints, they refuse medication and decompensate. Released addicts face an influx of choices they cannot handle. Given temptation, they revert to drug use and to crime. Such men need intermediate institutions until they evolve the resources to survive outside completely structured settings.

What Sort of Hybrid?

The uniqueness of a setting of the kind we have prescribed for our disturbed offenders lies in a combination of hospital-features and prison-features which it needs in pursuit of its mission.[19] The offenders we are concerned with (DVOs) must be placed in confinement because they have taken lives or injured people in the community; but they also require a mental health setting because they have long-standing problems.

How can a setting be neither prison nor hospital, and yet be both? We have already discussed some criteria or requisites, but we could add some others which have to do with combinations of attributes of prison and hospital:

We must make sure that clients qualify on all counts. The kind of setting we would institute must contain clearly disturbed offenders. The most plausible way to start is to replicate our sampling design, which asks whether the offenders of concern have histories of mental health problems. The next step is to find those offenders whose mental health problems are still alive or have resuscitated in prison. Mental health problems should be substantial but must fall short of requiring hospital commitment.

---

19. The art in designing a hybrid setting is to link the most desirable features of component settings. If one links the least admirable features (such as the way medication is used as treatment in hospitals and the emphasis on conformity in prisons) one can harm inmates and damage the system. This principle of designing composites was captured by Bernard Shaw, who was asked by an actress to father a child that could combine her appearance with his intelligence. "But madam," Shaw said (or words to that effect), "what if the child had my looks and your brains?"

We must make sure the clients match the setting. One matching issue revolves around the severity of mental health problems with which a setting can deal. The more substantial the representation of mental health staff in a setting, the more serious the problems it can address. It does not matter in this connection whether the administrative umbrella of a program is corrections, mental health, or conjoint, but whether staffing levels are sufficiently rich. (For example, it is to be assumed that medication must be administered by nurses, under medical supervision). A second matching issue has to do with security concerns. Some disturbed offenders are dangerous, some are victim-prone, and others combine predatory and vulnerable features. A setting that contains such persons must be able to separate them so they pose no danger to each other, and it must provide sufficient coverage to prevent victimization.

We must make sure clients get the benefit of helpful prison features. We have noted that one advantage of prisons over hospitals lies in the educational, training, and work opportunities they try to provide. This is a normalizing feature which can be adopted to good effect in hybrid settings. Programing is particularly helpful in providing respectable content around which inmates and staff (and inmates in groups) can relate to each other.[20]

20. In a classic study of federal prisons Glaser found that work supervisors had rehabilitative effects upon inmates far out of proportion to their numbers (D. Glaser, *The Effectiveness of a Prison and Parole System* [Indianapolis: Bobbs-Merrill, 1964]). These findings document a listing of requisites for constructive prison impact, which would include that

1. The place where change occurs has dominant or salient work to be done (such as plumbing, carpentry, running Sunday school, or clerking for a guard) which frames a relationship that is a vehicle for change.
2. If possible, a legitimizing peer ingroup develops which approves of staff/inmate links and/or
3. The staff and inmate(s) are ecologically insulated from pressures that emanate from the prison-at-large.
4. Staff-inmate links shift from instrumental task orientation to links featuring supportiveness, warmth and loyalty, permitting modeling, emulation, and spontaneous influence (H. Toch, "Psychological treatment of imprisoned offenders," in J. R. Hays, T. K. Roberts, and K. S. Solway, eds., *Violence and the Violent Individual* [New York: Spectrum, 1981], 230. See also, H. Toch, "Regenerating prisoners through education," *Federal Probation*, 1987, *51*, 61–66)

A second feature of interest to us is that prisons are cafeterias of settings that can be used as substitutes or supplements in designing a well-rounded program. During the day an inmate could attend a specialized group or a regular shop setting. He could also be segregated or isolated if he needs time to be alone and regroup. *We must make sure the inmate gets the benefit of hospital components.* We have alluded to the fact that prison regimes are rigid. Prisons treat a wide range of behavior lapses as rule violations. Dispositions—which are punitive—vary with the severity of the infraction, rather than with the expected impact of dispositions on future behavior. Hospital reactions to disruptive conduct are more personalized and more concerned with anticipated effects on the patient, including iatrogenic effects (which make the patient sicker).[21] This more personalized approach can be used in prisons for disturbed inmates where standard dispositions make the least sense or where they can do the greatest harm. Another practice worth emulating is that of mental health case management, which includes treatment planning, conferences that review progress, and revised programing contingent on observed behavior.

We must make sure the inmate gets the benefit of cross-fertilization. This point is probably most important, though least obvious. DVOs are multiproblem offenders, not because they are dis-

---

In referring to the therapeutic community inmate, Maxwell Jones observed,

> If his interest can be obtained in some simple and familiar work, and particularly if the occupational therapist can enter into a supportive relationship with him, even the most elementary occupation may be therapeutic; it may bring out and direct constructively a variety of emotions which have been denied outlet, and it may do something to offset the restrictions of the mental-hospital regime. . . . [an effectively utilized constructive work group] is capable of leading to better contact with reality, to behavior more in accordance with social standards, and to the foundations of self-esteem. (M. Jones, B. A. Pomryn, and E. Skellern, "Work therapy," *Lancet*, March 31, 1956, 343–44, p. 343).

21. R. F. Morgan, *The Iatrogenics Handbook* (Toronto: IPI Publishing, 1983). Glaser (*The Effectiveness of a Parole System*) is one of few students who argues that "let the punishment fit the crime" is an excessively rigid criterion for disciplining institutional transgressors.

turbed and violent, but because their problems are long-standing and complex. The same circumstance holds for many other offenders (and many patients) but plays a limited role in how we deal with them. If future approaches are to be better approaches the presumption is that they must be less monothematic than current strategies, using a wider range of interventions and expertise. The DVO's case is nonoptional, because he demands interdisciplinary confluence, interagency collaboration, and teaming in delivering services. The necessity of experimenting with interface arrangements forces us to evolve flexible models for responding to multiproblem clients with multiservice approaches. This is an exciting frontier for experimentation and innovation. For those in corrections who might participate and become parties to extending this frontier, it may be a source of adventure. And for many, it may be a way to make a difference, which is a rare experience in prisons.

Index

acting alone as offense characteristic, 62, 66, 67, 68
Adams, Ken, x
addiction. *See* substance abusers
adolescent offenders, 4. *See also* institutions *and individual types of offense*
ages of offenders, 48, 49*T*, 50, 58, 75, 93
agglomeration process, 46
alcohol: crimes committed under influence of, 32, 53, 113, 114, 118, 119, 127, 129, 131–32, 133, 134. *See also* psychiatric-substance abuse offenders; substance abusers
Alexander, Franz, 4
"Alternatives to Incarceration" proposal, 154*n*
antisocial personality disturbance, 4
arson, 37, 53, 61, 71, 90, 128–30
assault, 53, 61, 62, 68
automobiles. *See* vehicular violence

background of inmates. *See* criminal histories; social variables *and individual types of offense*

Bazelon, J., 13
binary data, 45
Bronner, Augusta, 4
burglars, 37, 53, 54, 61, 66; impulsive, 75, 78, 79; dependent, 93–95; addicted, 100, 102–03; inexperienced, 107, 110; experienced, 110–12
"bus therapy," 166*n*

"career-based typologies," 27
career concept, 40–46, 47, 71; offender career patterns, 54–55, 56*T*, 57, 58*T*, 59*T*
case studies: use of, 3, 4–5, 7. *See also individual types of offense*
cause and effect sequences, 27
child abuse, 70, 87, 105; offenders as victims of, 79, 86; sex crimes against, 86, 112, 135, 136
chronicity of criminal violence, 27, 55, 57, 58, 119
civil libertarians, 159
civil psychiatric patients, 32
clinical science, 3, 7–8

179